HAWAI'I'S BEST *mochi* RECIPES

Library of Congress Catalog Card
Number: 00-105565

First Printing, September 2000
Second Printing, November 2000
Third Printing, May 2001
Fourth Printing, March 2002
Fifth Printing, November 2003
Sixth Printing, May 2004
Seventh Printing, August 2006
7 8 9

Design by Jane Hopkins
Photography by Ray Wong

ISBN-10: 1-56647-336-5
ISBN-13: 978-1-56647-336-1

Mutual Publishing, LLC
1215 Center Street, Suite 210
Honolulu, Hawaii 96816
Ph: (808) 732-1709
Fax: (808) 734-4094
e-mail: info@mutualpublishing.com
www.mutualpublishing.com

Printed in Korea

HAWAI'I'S BEST *mochi* RECIPES

Jean Watanabe Hee

MUTUAL PUBLISHING

Dedication

This cookbook is dedicated to my mother, Asae Watanabe, who made me what I am today. She was my first teacher and has always been there for me. Thanks, mom, for your love and support in everything I do.

Acknowledgments

To my friends and relatives who contributed to my collection of recipes throughout the years.

To Amy and Evie, my sisters-in-law, who love to cook and have created and used their special touch to alter and improve recipes, and who willingly shared them with me.

To Mrs. Kay Yanagihara who, for more than 20 years, always provided her special treats for my family and me whenever we visited Hilo. And to all the rest of my mother's wonderful friends who also shared their tasty homemade goodies with us. Thanks for sharing your recipes with my mother who then shared them with me.

To my mother whose recipe collection (many of them handwritten) provided a rich source from which I began collecting all the mochi concoctions I could find.

To my husband, Don, who encouraged and supported me in this project.

Table of Contents

Why Mochi?

Growing up in Hilo, I was part of a large Japanese community. We followed many of the traditions of Japan where my grandparents came from. Pounding mochi for the New Year was a huge event involving family and friends. As a little girl, I remember eagerly waiting for freshly made soft mochi filled with sweet "an" and the green speckled mochi flavored with yomogi. Even now mochi in any form is a treat for me.

On New Year's Day, as part of our tradition, my mother always prepared ozoni soup with a soft mochi in it for each of us. Eating mochi as our first meal for the New Year would bring us good health and good luck.

On cold Hilo nights, hardened mochi became a late snack when it was fried, crisp and brown on the outside and soft in the middle and then rolled in kinako and sugar.

My grandmother even made homemade kakimochi which I loved. Sesame seeds were pounded into the mochi and after the mochi hardened a little it was cut into thin strips and dried in the sun for days. When thoroughly dried, the strips were fried in oil, where they would puff up, light and crispy. With sugar sprinkled over, delicious!

Today there is so much more to mochi. There are many tasty contributions from the diverse ethnic groups in Hawai'i with their own special recipes and traditions. Everyone enjoys mochi's special texture and chewiness, and over the years my collection of mochi recipes grew, thanks especially to my mother and her friends in Hilo, all great cooks.

My mother still makes ozoni. Recently I've learned to prepare it her way, with lots of vegetables. I'd like my daughters, fourth generation in Hawai'i to remember visiting Hilo, with all the cousins sleeping on the living room floor on futons, with grandpa preparing the fireplace for a marshmallow roast and Linny calling out, "Grandma, can we please have fried mochi with kinako?" And maybe, someday, they'll prepare ozoni and fried mochi for their grandchildren.

This recipe is the way my mother makes it and it's delicious. I like all the vegetables that add to the soup's flavor.

Mom's Ozoni

8 cups water

1/2 cup dried shrimps

3-4 shiitake mushrooms, soaked, sliced thin

1/4 cup gobo, scraped clean and slivered (Soak in water to prevent discoloration.)

1/4 cup carrots, slivered

2 strips nishime konbu, washed and tied in knots about 2 inches apart. Cut between knots.

2 cups mizuna, cut into one-inch lengths

2 tablespoons shoyu

1 teaspoon salt

Kamaboko, sliced

Mochi, whole or small pieces

Place shrimps in cold water, bring to boil and simmer over low heat for 20-25 minutes. Strain. Place broth back on stove and discard shrimps. Add sliced mushrooms, gobo, carrots and konbu. Simmer on medium heat until vegetables are tender (about 5-10 minutes) Add mizuna. Add shoyu and salt to taste. Simmer on low heat Place fresh mochi and 2-3 kamaboko slices into soup bowl and pour soup over.

Note: If desired, drop fresh mochi into soup briefly to soften. If mochi has hardened, cook in hot water in a separate saucepan to desired softness before placing in soup bowl.

Linny's Favorite

1 mochi per person
oil for frying
1/2 cup kinako
1/2 cup sugar

Heat about a tablespoon of oil in frying pan. Fry mochi on low heat until lightly browned on both sides. Sprinkle a few drops of water, cover pan and cook for a minute more. Mix kinako and sugar together. Remove mochi and coat with kinako mixture.

Note: Fresh mochi pounded for New Year's may be frozen and later eaten this way. If thawed mochi feels very hard, soak in water for desired softness. Pat dry before frying. Hot mochi can be very sticky. Use caution when eating.

In our swiftly changing technological society, many now use mochi machines which can steam and knead the sweet rice into mochi. Each mochi machine comes with specific instructions and is simple to use. The mochi is similar in texture to traditionally pounded mochi. (It is recommended that you do purchase quality sweet rice for better flavor.)

Traditional Mochi

There are still families in Hawai'i following the custom of pounding mochi just before New Year's Eve. They gather together for fellowship and tradition and also in the belief that this helps to perpetuate good fortune and long life.

For those interested in the traditional way you may need to look for the following equipment:

Usu	carved out stone bowl used to pound the steamed sweet rice
Kine	wooden mallets used to pound the rice

Seiro	wooden boxes used to steam the sweet rice
Wooden mats	used in the wooden boxes so rice can be easily steamed

Step 1:

Wash 5 pounds of sweet rice until water runs clear. Cover rice with water and soak overnight. Change water once.

Step 2:

Drain rice and spread evenly over wooden mats in seiro. Steam for about 45 minutes over rapidly boiling water until rice becomes tender and translucent. (While steaming, sprinkle water over rice about three times.)

Step 3:

Prepare the usu (stone bowl) with hot water. Drain the hot water before putting in steamed rice. Mash the rice with the kine (wooden mallet) dipped in water. After mashing, begin pounding.

Step 4:

A person, named the Mixer, turns the mochi during the mashing and pounding for even pounding of the mochi. He also determines when the mochi is done.

Step 5:

Place mochi on board sprinkled with katakuriko (potato starch). Pinch off pieces to form plain mochi cakes or mochi may be filled with tsubushi-an.

Note: The plain mochi cakes are used in Ozoni, the traditional New Year's Day soup. Different sizes of mochi are used for offerings in the home and in the Buddhist temples.

Helpful Hints

Mochi is pounded rice cake. When used in the title (like Butter Mochi) it means that some form of the sweet rice (flour or rice kernels)may be an ingredient.

Mochi rice is sweet rice, glutinous rice (rice kernels)

Mochiko is sweet rice flour, glutinous rice flour (powdered form)

1 box Mochiko = 1 pound =16 ounces = 3 cups

1 package Mochiko = 10 ounces = 2 cups

Purchase either boxes or packages of Mochiko as directed by recipe's directions for easy measuring.

Use a plastic knife for cutting mochi, baked mochi desserts, etc.

Do not put baked mochi in freezer or refrigerator.

Baked mochi keeps for a few days without refrigeration.

Prepare mochi dessert a day ahead to let it set.

Store cooled mochi desserts in a loose-lidded container for 2-3 days in warm weather, up to 5 days in cool weather.

Leftover Koshian (bean paste) may be frozen until needed again.

Freeze plain pounded mochi cakes in an airtight container

To soften hardened mochi, soak in water.

MEMORABLE *mochi* DESSERTS

An Mochi #1

2 cups mochiko (10-oz pkg)
1/2 cup sugar
2 cups water
1 can koshian (12-oz can)
katakuriko (potato starch) for sprinkling

Boil water and sugar together. Remove from stove. Pour mochiko into syrup and stir vigorously until dough is free of lumps. Sprinkle potato starch on cutting board. Turn cooked mochi on board. If too hot, allow to cool. Pinch off large walnut size (1-1/2") pieces of dough, then flatten and shape to form 3-1/2" round wrappers. Place one teaspoon or more koshian in middle. Gather edges together and shape into a ball. Lay pinched side down.

An Mochi #2

2-1/2 cups mochiko
1-1/4 cups brown sugar
1 teaspoon baking powder
1 can coconut milk (12-oz)
1-1/2 cups water
3/4 cup koshian
katakuriko or kinako for sprinkling

Combine mochiko, brown sugar and baking powder. Add coconut milk, water and koshian and mix until well blended. Pour into greased 9 x 13 inch pan and bake at 325° for 1 hour. Cool before cutting.

Sprinkle and roll in katakuriko.

Apricot Mochi

yield: 24-32 pieces

1 pound mochiko (16-oz box)
2 apricot-flavored gelatin (3-oz box)
1 can apricot nectar (12-oz)
12-oz water (use nectar can)
1-1/4 cups sugar
katakuriko (potato starch) for sprinkling

Combine all ingredients except katakuriko and mix thoroughly with whisk or spoon. Pour into a 9 x 13 inch greased pan. Cover tightly with foil and bake at 350° for 55 minutes. Cool with cover on for 15 minutes. Remove foil and cool for several hours before cutting with a plastic knife. Coat with potato starch.

Baduya Karabasa

4 cups mochiko (2 10-oz pkgs)
3/4 cup brown sugar
1 cup squash or pumpkin, cooked and shredded
2-3 cups coconut milk
oil for deep frying

Mix together mochiko, sugar and squash. Stir coconut milk in gradually to the mixture to make a soft dough. Heat oil. Drop mixture by tablespoonful into the hot oil. Cook until done and light golden brown.

Baked Mochi #1

1 pound mochiko (16-oz box)
2 1/2 cups sugar
1 teaspoon baking powder
2 cups water (3tbsp)
1 can coconut milk (12-oz) (13.5 oz can)
1 teaspoon vanilla
food color, red or green

Mix dry ingredients in large mixing bowl. Add water and coconut milk gradually until well mixed. Add vanilla and a few drops of food color. Pour into greased 9 x 13 inch pan. Cover tightly with foil. Place pan in center of oven. Bake at 325° for 1 hour. Uncover and cool for several hours.

Baked Mochi #2

4 cups mochiko (2-10 oz pkgs)
1 teaspoon baking soda
2 cups brown sugar
1 cup white sugar
2 teaspoons white sesame seeds
1 can coconut milk (12-oz)
2-1/2 cups fresh milk
2 teaspoons vanilla

Mix all ingredients in a large bowl until batter is smooth. Pour into 9 x 13 inch ungreased pan. Bake at 350° for 45-50 minutes. Cool before cutting.

Baked Rice Pudding Thai-Style

6 ounces mochi rice
2 tablespoons light brown sugar
2 cups coconut milk, divided
1 cup water
3 eggs
2 tablespoons sugar

In a saucepan, combine mochi rice, brown sugar, 1 cup of the coconut milk and 1 cup water. Bring to a boil; simmer for 15-20 minutes or until the rice has absorbed most of the liquid. Stir from time to time.

Preheat oven to 300 degrees. Place rice mixture into a large ovenproof dish. Mix together in a bowl: eggs, the remaining 1 cup coconut milk and sugar. Strain and pour over rice. Place the dish in a baking pan. Pour boiling water into the pan up to half the height of the dish. Cover with foil. Bake for 35-55 minutes or until the rice pudding is set. Serve warm or cold.

Bibingka #1

yield: 24-32 pieces

4 cups mochiko (2 10-oz pkgs)
2 teaspoons baking powder
1 can coconut milk (12-oz)
3 cups fresh milk
1 teaspoon vanilla
1/2 cup butter
3 cups sugar
4 eggs

Mix together mochiko and baking powder and set aside. Stir together in a bowl coconut milk, fresh milk and vanilla. In a large bowl cream butter and sugar. Add eggs, one at a time and beat well after each addition. Add alternately into the creamed mixture, the mochiko mixture and the milk mixture. Mix thoroughly until smooth. Pour into greased 9 x 13 inch pan. Bake 350° for 1 hour. Cool before cutting.

Bibingka #2

4-1/2 cups mochiko
2-1/2 teaspoons baking powder
3 cups sugar
4 cups milk
1/2 cup butter, melted
5 eggs

Mix dry ingredients in a large mixing bowl. In a separate bowl, lightly beat eggs and add milk and butter. Gradually add this mixture to the dry ingredients and stir until smooth. Pour batter into greased 9x13 inch pan. Bake at 350° for 45 minutes or until golden brown.

Bibingka #3

1 pound mochiko (16-oz box)
3/4 cup sugar
1 cup milk
3 eggs, beaten
2 cans coconut milk (2 12-oz)
1 tablespoon vanilla

Combine mochiko and sugar. Add milk and eggs. Add coconut milk and vanilla and mix thoroughly. Pour into a greased 9 x 13 inch pan. Bake at 350° for 1 hour. Cool before cutting.

Biko

2-1/2 pounds Mochi rice
1 cup coconut milk, divided
1/2 cup dark brown sugar
1/2 cup light Brown sugar

Rinse mochi rice; drain. Repeat until water runs clear. Place in rice cooker. Add enough water to cover 1" over rice level. Cook

In a saucepan, combine coconut milk with sugar and cook over low heat until thick. Reserve 1/2 cup milk mixture and add remainder to cooked rice. Pour into a 9 x 13 inch pan lined with foil and press evenly. Brush reserved 1/2cup milk mixture over rice and bake at 350° for 20-25 minutes. Cool and cut.

Blueberry Mochi

yield: about 36 pieces

1 pound mochiko (16-oz box)
1 cup butter, melted
2 cups sugar
1 can evaporated millk (12-oz can)
4 eggs
2 teaspoons baking powder
2 teaspoons vanilla
1 can blueberry pie filling

Stir sugar in melted butter. Add milk and mix well. Add eggs and mix. Stir in baking powder, mochiko and vanilla. Pour into ungreased 9 x 13 inch pan. Fold in the blueberry pie filling creating a marbleized look. Bake at 350° for 1 hour or until toothpick tests clean.

Bud Bud (Filipino Rice Pudding)

6 cups Mochi rice (soak about 2 hours)
1 box dark brown sugar (save some to sprinkle on rice)
1 can coconut milk (12-oz)
butter

Cook rice with 7 cups of water. Simmer brown sugar and coconut milk until sugar dissolves. Mix into cooked rice. Grease 13 x 11 pan, or spray with Pam. Press rice evenly into pan. Sprinkle some brown sugar and butter on top. Bake at 400° for 30 minutes. Leave overnight covered with a clean dish cloth.

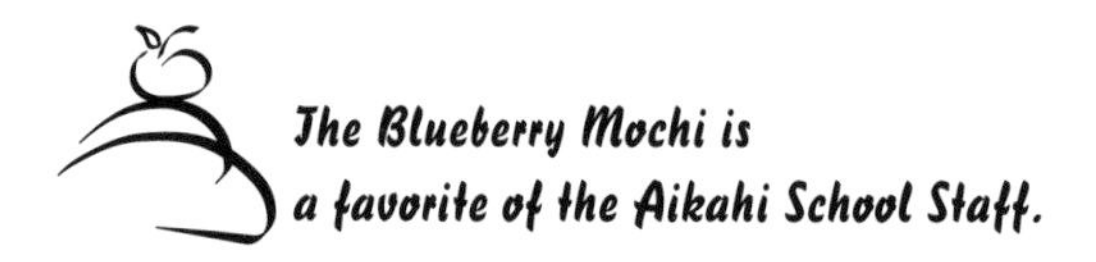

The Blueberry Mochi is a favorite of the Aikahi School Staff.

Bunuelos

2 cups mochiko (10-oz pkg)
1 cup coconut, grated
1/4 cup sugar
1 teaspoon baking powder
pinch of salt
1 cup water
oil for frying
sugar for sprinkling

Mix mochiko, coconut, sugar, baking powder and salt. Add water gradually and mix until well blended. Consistency should not be too wet or too dry. Shape into balls and fry for 10 minutes or until brown. Drain. Roll in or sprinkle with sugar.

Butter Mochi #1

1 pound mochiko (16-oz box)
3 cups sugar
1 tablespoon baking powder
1/2 cup butter or margarine
5 eggs, beaten
1 teaspoon vanilla
1 can coconut milk (12-oz)

Melt butter and set aside to cool. In large mixing bowl, combine all ingredients. Mix with spoon until batter is smooth. Pour into well greased 9 x 13 inch pan. Bake at 375° for 1 hour or until toothpick comes out clean. Cool and cut into squares.

Butter Mochi #2

1 pound mochiko (16-oz box)
2 cups sugar
2 teaspoons baking powder
2 cups milk
1/2 cup butter, melted
5 eggs
1 teaspoon vanilla
1 can coconut milk (12-oz)

Combine and mix dry ingredients in large mixing bowl. Add in remaining ingredients. Use a wire whisk to mix thoroughly until batter is smooth. Pour into 9 x 13 inch pan, greased or sprayed with Pam. Bake at 350° for 1 hour.

Butter Mochi #3

1 pound mochiko (16-oz box)
1/3 cup butter
2-1/4 cups sugar
4 eggs
2 teaspoons baking powder
1 teaspoon vanilla
1 can evaporated milk (12-oz)
1 can coconut milk (13.5-oz)

Cream butter and sugar in mixing bowl. To evaporated milk, add water to make 2 cups liquid. Add liquid and rest of ingredients into the mixing bowl and stir well for a smooth batter. Pour into lightly greased or sprayed 9 x 13 inch pan. Bake at 350° for 1 hour. Cool and cut with plastic knife.

Cascaron #1

1 pound mochiko (16-oz box)
1 pkg sweetened, flaked coconut (14-oz)
2 cups water
oil for deep frying
16 wooden skewers
syrup (1 cup sugar and 2 tablespoons water)

Mix mochiko with coconut and the 2 cups water. Shape into 1-1/4 inch balls. Heat oil to 350°. Fry mochi balls until golden brown. Drain on paper towels. Thread 3 cascaron on each skewer. In a saucepan, combine sugar and the 2 tablespoons water. Cook until sugar is completely dissolved and syrup reaches the "soft ball stage" (236° F on a candy thermometer.) Drizzle over cascaron.

Cascaron #2

2 cups mochiko (10-oz pkg)
2 cups grated coconut
1/2 cup sugar
1 teaspoon baking powder
1/2 teaspoon salt
1 cup evaporated milk (or enough to moisten)
oil for frying
sugar for sprinkling

Mix mochiko, sugar, baking powder and salt. Add coconut and mix. Stir milk into dry ingredients until very moist. Drop by teaspoonfuls in hot oil (280° - 300°.) Fry until light brown. Drain. Drop into a bag of sugar and shake to coat cascaron.

Chi Chi Dango (Baked)

1 pound mochiko (16-oz box)
2-1/4 cups sugar
1-1/2 teaspoons baking powder
1-1/2 cups water
1 can coconut milk (12-oz)
food color (optional)

Combine dry ingredients in large mixing bowl. Add liquid ingredients and mix thoroughly with whisk. Pour into greased 9 x 13 inch pan. Cover with foil and bake at 350° for 1 hour. Remove foil and cool thoroughly for at least 3-4 hours. Cut with plastic knife.

Chi Chi Mochi (Steamed)

2 cups mochiko (10-oz pkg)
1-1/4 cups water
1-3/4 cups sugar
1/2 cup water
food color, red or green
1 teaspoon vanilla
katakuriko (potato starch)

Mix mochiko and 1-1/4 cups water and roll into ball. Place ball in damp cloth and steam for 30-40 minutes. Cook sugar with 1/2 cup water until sugar is dissolved. Add a few drops of red or green coloring. Mix into cooked mochi and add vanilla. Mix and pour into flat pan sprinkled with katakuriko. Smooth. Cool before cutting.

Chien Doi (Chinese Doughnuts)

1-1/2 cups Chinese brown sugar (or regular brown sugar)
1-1/4 cups water
1 pound mochiko (16-oz box)
1 teaspoon sherry

Filling:
1/2 cup grated coconut, unsweetened
1/2 cup roasted peanuts, crushed
3 tablespoons sugar
1/4 cup sesame seeds, toasted
oil for deep frying

Dissolve brown sugar in hot water. When cool, stir gradually into mochiko to make a stiff dough (do not knead). Add sherry. Shape into a roll, 1-1/2 inches in diameter. Cut into 1/2 inch slices and flatten.

Combine filling ingredients and place a tablespoon of filling in center. Pinch edges together to seal and roll into a ball. Roll in sesame seeds. Deep fry in hot oil until golden brown. Press balls against side of pan while frying so balls will expand. Drain on paper towels.

Chinese Mochi

5 cups mochiko
1 box dark brown sugar
1 can coconut milk (12-oz)
1 teaspoon baking soda
sesame seeds for top

To coconut milk, add enough water to make 4 cups of liquid. Mix together all ingredients except sesame seeds. Blend until batter is smooth. Pour into 1 layer cake-size pan. Sprinkle sesame seeds on top. Bake for 1 hour at 325°. Cool before cutting.

Chocolate Mochi

2 cups mochiko (10-oz pkg)
2 cups sugar
1 tablespoon baking soda
1/2 cup butter or margarine
1 cup semi-sweet chocolate chips
2 cans evaporated milk (2 12-oz)
2 teaspoons vanilla
2 eggs, beaten

Sift mochiko, sugar and baking soda in a large bowl. Melt butter and chocolate chips together and combine with milk, vanilla and eggs. Mix well and stir into dry ingredients. Mix thoroughly until batter is smooth. Pour into greased 9 x 13 inch pan. Bake at 350° for 45-55 minutes. Cool. Cut with a plastic knife.

Cocoa Mochi

yield: 60 small pieces

2 cups mochiko (10-oz pkg)
1-3/4 cups sugar
3 tablespoons cocoa
1 tablespoon baking soda
2 eggs
1 can evaporated milk (12-oz)
1 can coconut milk (12-oz)
1/4 cup butter, melted
2 teaspoons vanilla

Sift together mochiko, sugar, cocoa and baking soda in a large mixing bowl. In another bowl, lightly beat eggs and add evaporated milk, coconut milk, butter and vanilla and mix. Pour into dry ingredients and mix until batter is smooth. Pour batter into greased 9 x 13 inch pan. Bake at 350° for 1 hour 10 minutes. Cool completely.

Coconut Azuki Mochi

5 cups mochiko
2-1/4 cups brown sugar
2 cans coconut milk (2 12-oz)
1 can water (use coconut milk can)
1 teaspoon baking soda
1 can tsubushian (18-oz)
1 tablespoon sesame seeds

Mix all ingredients except the sesame seeds. Pour into greased 9 x 13 inch pan. Sprinkle sesame seeds over mixture. Bake at 350° for 1 hour and 15 minutes or until toothpick comes out clean. Cool. Cut into bars with a plastic knife.

Coconut Butter Mochi

1 pound mochiko (16-oz box)

3 cups sugar

1 tablespoon baking powder

1/2 cup butter or margarine, melted

1 can coconut milk (12-oz)

1 teaspoon coconut extract

2 cups fresh milk

5 eggs, beaten

1 teaspoon vanilla

Topping:

2 tablespoons butter or margarine

1/4 cup sugar

1/8 cup kinako

sesame seeds

Combine all ingredients, except topping, and mix well. Pour into greased 9 x 13 inch pan and bake at 350° for 1 hour. Halfway through the baking time, remove pan from oven and sprinkle topping over the mochi. Return to oven and finish baking. Cool.

Coconut Custard Mochi

4 cups mochiko (2 10-oz pkgs.)
1/2 cup butter
3 cups sugar
4 eggs
3 teaspoons baking powder
1 can coconut milk (12-oz)
1 can evaporated milk (13-oz)
2 teaspoons vanilla

Beat butter and sugar. Use electric mixer. Add eggs and beat well. Add water to coconut milk to make 2 cups liquid. Also add water to evaporated milk to make 2 cups liquid. Put all the milk, mochi flour, baking powder and vanilla into the creamed mixture and mix well. Pour batter into greased and floured 9 x 13 inch pan. Bake at 350° for 1 hour.

Optional: Sprinkle toasted sesame seeds over batter before baking.

Coconut Mochi #1

4 cups mochiko (2 10-oz pkgs)
3-1/2 cups sugar
2 teaspoons baking powder
4 eggs, beaten
1/2 cup butter, melted
1 can coconut milk (12-oz)
1 can evaporated milk (12-oz)
1 teaspoon vanilla

Mix together dry ingredients in large mixing boil. To evaporated milk add water to make 4 cups liquid. Add liquid and rest of wet ingredients to dry ingredients. Blend until smooth. Pour into greased 9 x 13 inch pan. Bake at 325° for 1 hour and 10 minutes, or until golden brown. Cool and cut into pieces.

Coconut Mochi #2

4 cups mochiko (2 10-oz pkgs)
1 box light brown sugar
1 can coconut milk (12-oz)
1 tablespoon baking soda
sesame seeds
katakuriko (potato starch) for sprinkling

To coconut milk, add enough water to make 4 cups liquid. Add mochiko, brown sugar and baking soda and mix well until batter is smooth. Pour into well-buttered 9 x 13 inch pan. Sprinkle sesame seeds on top and bake at 350°for 45-60 minutes. Cool overnight. Cut with a plastic knife. Roll in katakuriko.

Variation 1: Add 1 can prepared tsubushian or chopped walnuts.

Coconut Mochi Dessert

2 cups mochiko (10-oz pkg)
1 cup brown sugar
1 cup white sugar
1 tablespoon baking powder
1/4 teaspoon salt
2 eggs
1/4 cup butter, melted and slightly cooled
1 can evaporated milk (13-oz)
1 cup shredded coconut
1/3 cup finely chopped walnuts

Mix mochiko, sugar, salt and baking powder in large bowl. Beat eggs in small bowl and add evaporated milk and melted butter. Pour into dry ingredients and blend. Add coconut and nuts. Pour into 9 x 13 inch ungreased pan. Bake 45 minutes at 350°

Coconut Mochi Squares

1 pound mochiko (16-oz box)
2 cups sugar
1 teaspoon baking powder
1 can evaporated milk (13-oz)
1 can water (use milk can)
3 eggs
1/4 cup butter or margarine, melted
2 teaspoons vanilla
1-1/2 cups flaked coconut

Mix mochiko, sugar and baking powder together. In another bowl, beat eggs slightly and mix in milk and water. Stir in melted butter.

Mix liquid and dry ingredients together. Blend thoroughly so batter is smooth. Add vanilla and 1 cup coconut. Pour into two greased 11 x 7 inch pans. Let stand about 15 minutes. Sprinkle balance of coconut on top. Cover pans with foil. Bake in 350° oven (covered for 45 minutes and uncovered 15 minutes. Cool thoroughly and cut into squares.

Coconut Nantu

5 cups mochiko
2-3/4 cups brown sugar
1 teaspoon baking soda
1 can coconut milk (12-oz)
2-1/2 cups water
sesame seeds (optional)

Mix dry ingredients together. Add coconut milk and water and mix well. Pour into greased 9 x 13 inch pan. Sprinkle with sesame seeds if desired. Bake at 350° for 50-55 minutes. Let stand at least 6 hours before cutting.

Coconut Rice Cake

4 cups mochiko (2 10-oz pkgs)
1 tablespoon baking powder
4 cups coconut milk
1-1/2 cups brown sugar
1 teaspoon vanilla
1 banana leaf, cleaned and cut into approximately 11 x 15 inch pieces
coconut milk for brushing

Mix mochiko and baking powder. Gradually add 4 cups coconut milk and blend together. Add sugar and vanilla; mix until batter is smooth.

Line 9 x 13 inch pan with 2-3 layers of banana leaves. Trim leaves at rim of pan. Brush coconut milk on leaves. Pour mochiko batter into pan and bake at 300° for 20 minutes. Remove pan from oven and brush coconut milk on mochi surface. Return to oven and bake for 1 hour. (Total baking time: 1 hour and 20 minutes)

Coconut-Sweet Potato Patty

4 cups mochiko (2 10-oz pkgs)
1 cup brown sugar (loosely packed)
2-1/2 cups coconut milk
1 cup sweet potatoes (grated or shredded)
oil for frying

Mix mochiko, sugar and sweet potatoes together. Gradually add coconut milk to make a soft dough. Heat some oil in frying pan. Drop dough by tablespoons and cook until both sides are brown.

Coffee Chi Chi Mochi

2 cups mochiko (10-oz pkg)
1-1/4 cups milk
2 cups sugar
1/2 cup Kona coffee, strong
1/2 cup katakuriko (potato starch)

Combine mochiko and milk to form a dough. Wrap in damp cloth and steam for 30 to 40 minutes. Heat coffee and sugar until sugar is completely dissolved. Add hot syrup mixture to steamed dough and blend well. Work quickly as mixture will be lumpy if allowed to cool. Quickly pour into large pan sprinkled with katakuriko. Cool. Cut into desired shape with a plastic knife.

Custard Mochi #1

4 cups mochiko (2 10-oz pkgs)
1/2 cup butter
2-1/2 cups sugar
4 eggs
3 teaspoons baking powder
4 cups evaporated milk
2 teaspoons vanilla

Beat together butter and sugar. Add eggs and mix well. Add mochiko, baking powder, milk and vanilla. Mix thoroughly until smooth. Grease and flour 9 x 13 inch pan. Bake at 350° for 1 hour. Cool and cut.

Custard Mochi #2

2 cups mochiko (10-oz pkg)
1/2 cup butter, melted
1-1/2 cups sugar
4 eggs, beaten
3 teaspoons baking powder
4 cups milk
2 teaspoons vanilla

Blend together butter, sugar and eggs. Add mochiko and baking powder and mix well. Add milk and vanilla. Mix batter until smooth. Pour into buttered and floured 9 x 13 inch pan. Bake at 350° for 1 hour.

Custard Poi Mochi

4 cups mochiko (2 10-oz pkgs)
1 cup butter, melted
1 pound poi, undiluted
4 eggs
1 can evaporated milk (12-oz)
2 cups sugar
1 tablespoon baking powder

Gradually mix milk into poi until well blended. Beat in eggs and butter. Stir in sugar, mochiko and baking powder and mix thoroughly. Pour into greased and floured 9 x 13 inch pan. Bake at 350° for 1 hour. Cool and cut with plastic knife.

Daifuku

1 cup mochiko
1/2 cup sugar
1 cup water, boiling
1 can tsubushian (18-oz)
katakuriko (potato starch) for sprinkling

Shape tsubushian into walnut-size balls (refrigerate if too soft to handle). Dissolve sugar into boiling water. Pour liquid into mochiko and mix well with a wooden spoon. Line steamer with clean, damp dishtowel or cheesecloth. Place mixture in steamer. Steam for 25 minutes. Remove from steamer onto board floured with katakuriko. Cool 1 to 2 minutes. Break off into golf ball-sized pieces and flatten in palm of hand leaving a shallow well in center. Put tsubushian ball in center of dough and bring edges of dough up and around. Pinch tightly to close.

Dau Lau

2 cups mochiko (10-oz pkg)
3/4 to 1 cup water
3/4 cup peanuts, chopped
3/4 cup coconut, grated or shredded
1/3 cup sesame seeds
1/2 cup sugar

Mix together peanuts, coconut, sesame seeds and sugar and set aside for topping. Mix mochiko and water together to form a dough. Pinch pieces of dough to form balls 1 inch in diameter. Place mochi balls in pot of boiling water. Bring to boil again and simmer for 5 to 8 minutes or until balls float to the top. Remove and drain on paper towel. Roll mochi balls in the topping mixture.

Dila-Dila

2 cups mochiko (10-oz pkg)
1/2 cup sugar
1 teaspoon baking powder
dash of salt
1 cup water
2 cups coconut, freshly grated
sugar for sprinkling
sesame seeds for sprinkling

Combine mochiko, sugar, baking powder and salt. Slowly add enough water to make a stiff dough. Shape dough into 1-1/2 inch balls. Flatten each ball into a patty. Drop several pieces at a time into a pot of boiling water. Cook until patties float. Remove and place in colander. Run under cold water; drain. Coat with coconut. Before serving, sprinkle with sugar and sesame seeds.

Easy Chinese Gao

6 cups mochiko
2 cans coconut milk (2 12-oz)
1 pound brown sugar
1 can yams (1 pound)
1/2 teaspoon baking powder
1/4 teaspoon vanilla
sesame seeds

To 2 cans coconut milk, add enough water to make 4 cups liquid. Heat over double-boiler. Dissolve brown sugar in hot milk. In a large mixing bowl, mash yams. Add milk mixture and mochiko alternately to yams. Add baking powder and vanilla. Blend well.

Place a pan of water on lower shelf of oven before preheating oven to bake at 350°

Line foil in greased 9 x 13 inch pan. Spread mixture evenly in pan. Sprinkle sesame seeds and cover pan with foil. Bake for 2 hours. Let stand for 24 hours or longer before cutting.

Filipino Coconut Rice Pudding

5-1/2 cups Mochi rice
5-1/2 cups water
1 can coconut milk (12-oz)
1 pound dark brown sugar, divided
banana leaves, cleaned

Rinse rice; drain. Cook rice with water in a rice cooker. In a saucepan, cook coconut milk and 1-1/4 cups of the brown sugar for about 20 minutes (medium heat) stirring constantly until mixture thickens. Wilt banana leaves by passing leaves through boiling water a few minutes. Line a 9 x 13 inch pan with the wilted banana leaves.

Put cooked rice into a large bowl. Reserving 1/2 cup of the milk mixture, stir the remainder and the remaining brown sugar into the hot rice. Mix well and put into lined pan. Pour the reserved 1/2 cup of the coconut milk mixture over rice. Bake at 350° for 20 minutes, then broil for 5 minutes to brown top. Cut into small pieces.

Fortune Cookies

yield: 25 fortune cookies

1 cup cake flour (like Softasilk), sifted
3 tablespoons mochiko
1/2 cup sugar
1/4 teaspoon salt
3 egg whites
1/4 cup vegetable oil
1/4 cup water
1 teaspoon vanilla
25 paper fortune strips, 1/2" X 2-1/2"

Combine cake flour, mochiko, sugar and salt in a bowl; set aside. In a large bowl, beat oil, egg whites, water and vanilla on medium speed for 1 minute. Mix in dry ingredients and blend until smooth. Drop 1 tablespoon batter onto a lightly oiled cookie sheet. Spread batter in a circular motion (use spoon bottom) to a 4 inch round circle. Bake 15-20 minutes at 325 degrees or until light brown. Remove cookies one at a time from oven. (Wear cloth gloves if too hot to handle.) Place a paper fortune strip on cookie, fold cookie in half and quickly bend the length of cookie over the edge of an empty can or similar object. Place the bent fortune cookie in a muffin pan to keep bent shape.

Note: Bake only a few cookies at a time for easier handling. If cookies harden before folding, reheat in oven.

Fried Bananas with Mochiko

3 tablespoons mochiko
1/4 cups sugar
2 eggs, beaten
8 firm bananas, ripe
1 cup shredded coconut
1/4 cup butter

Combine mochiko, sugar and eggs; mix well. Peel bananas and cut in half lengthwise, then in half crosswise. Dip bananas into mochiko mixture and coat generously. Roll in coconut. Heat butter in pan and saute bananas for 10 minutes, turning once. Serve hot.

Fried Mochi

1 pound mochiko (16-oz box)
1-1/4 cups sugar
1 teaspoon baking powder
3 tablespoons black sesame seeds
1-3/4 cups water
oil for frying

Mix mochiko, sugar, baking powder and sesame seeds. Add water until blended. Drop by spoonfuls into hot oil about 1/2 inches deep. Fry at medium to medium-high heat. Brown both sides of mochi until golden brown.

Gau #1 (Chinese New Year's Pudding)

1 pound mochiko
12 ounces Chinese brown sugar (or dark brown sugar)
2 cups boiling water
1 Hung jo (dried red date), optional
1 teaspoon sesame seeds

Dissolve sugar in boiling water. Set aside until cool enough to add mochiko. Add mochiko and blend thoroughly until smooth. Pour batter into lightly-greased, round cake pan. Place date in center and sprinkle with sesame seeds. Place pan in steamer and steam for 4-5 hours on high heat. (Begin on high setting; maintain on medium).

Gau #2

4 cups mochiko (2 10-oz pkgs)
3 cups brown sugar, packed firmly
3 cups water (including yam liquid)
1 can yam, mashed (16-oz)
3 tablespoons vegetable oil
toasted sesame seeds
3-4 ti leaves (remove thick rib section)

Dissolve sugar in boiling water. Add mashed yam. Cool thoroughly. Add mixture to mochiko, about half a cup at a time, mixing well after each addition. Pour into greased, ti leaf lined 9 x 13 inch pan. Cover tightly with foil. Place pan with batter on top shelf of oven and place a pan of water on lower shelf. Bake at 350° for 2 hours. Remove foil immediately after baking. Brush top with oil and sprinkle with toasted sesame seeds. Let stand for 2 days before cutting.

Gin Doi With Char Siu Filling

yield: about 20 doughnuts

Step 1: Filling

1 cup char siu, minced

1/4 cup dried baby shrimps, minced

1/4 cup chopped green onions

2 pieces shiitake mushrooms, soaked and minced

1/8 cup water chestnuts or bamboo shoots, minced

1-2 tablespoons oil

Heat pan and add oil. Stir-fry char siu and dried shrimps. Add mushrooms, green onions and water chestnuts; stir-fry 3-4 minutes. Set aside.

Step 2: Flour Mixture

3/4 cup sugar

1-1/4 cups water, or more as needed

2 teaspoons whiskey

1 pound mochiko (16-oz box)

Mix sugar and water until sugar is dissolved. Add whiskey and stir lightly. Place mochiko in a large bowl. Gradually add liquid mixture and stir until dough can be handled. (Add more mochiko or water if needed.) Knead dough until soft and firm.

Step 3: Forming Doughnuts

1/2 cup sesame seeds

1 quart oil (48 oz)

Pinch pieces of dough into golf ball size. Flatten dough and place about a tablespoon of filling in center of dough. Seal edges and shape into a ball. Roll in sesame seeds. Heat oil in wok or pot on medium heat until oil is very hot (375 degrees). Place about 4-5 doughnuts into oil. Turn and roll doughnuts until it begins to turn light brown. Press and flatten

continued on next page…

continued from previous page

doughnuts against side of wok, preferably using a wire mesh Chinese wok spoon. Continue to roll and press doughnuts. Doughnuts will double in size. After doughnuts float on top of oil, do not press and let doughnuts cook to a golden brown color. Remove from oil and drain on paper towels.

Thanks to Betty Leong for this Gin Doi recipe.

Guinataan

1 can coconut milk (32-oz)
1 cup mochiko
1 cup water
1/2 cup sugar
2 cups yams, cooked and sliced in 1/2-inch cubes
2 cups taro, cooked and sliced in 1/2-inch cubes
2 bananas (firm, ripe), peeled and cut in 1/2-inch slices

Mix 1/2 cup coconut milk with the mochiko to form a stiff dough. Shape into 1/2 inch balls; set aside. In a large saucepan combine remaining coconut milk, water and sugar. Cook over medium heat for 10 minutes, stirring occasionally. Add yams and mochiko balls. Cook for 10 minutes, stirring occasionally. Add taro and cook for 15 minutes or until desired thickness. Stir banana slices into pudding before serving.

Habutae Mochi

2-1/4 cups mochiko
1-1/3 cups water

Syrup:
1/2 cup sugar
1/4 cup water
1 can koshian (12-oz can)
food color, red or green
katakuriko (potato starch) for sprinkling

Mix mochiko and water lightly. Place on dampened dishcloth and steam for 10 minutes

Boil sugar and water on low heat until sugar is dissolved. Do not stir. Remove from heat and add 3-4 drops of food coloring. Put steamed mochi in a sturdy container and pound with a wooden spoon. Gradually add syrup, blending well while pounding. Place mochi on board dusted with katakuriko. Pinch off about 1 tablespoon of mochi and roll into a ball. Coat each ball with koshian.

Iga Mochi

1 pound mochiko (16-oz box)
1 cup flour
1/3 cup Wesson oil
1-3/4 cups water
1 can tsubushian (18-oz)
ti leaves (enough for 20 2-1/2" x 6" cut pieces)

Shape tsubushian into walnut size balls (refrigerate if too soft to handle) and set aside. Mix mochiko, flour, oil and water until the texture of bread dough. Pinch off a piece of mochi dough, flatten, and place tsubushian ball in center. Cover ball and pinch to seal. Place mochi in center of the cut piece of ti leaf. Fold both ends of leaf over mochi and place in steamer with leaf ends tucked under. May be stacked in steamer. Steam for 20 minutes. Discard leaf before eating.

Variation: Try avocado or fig leaves sprayed with Pam to wrap mochi.

Japanese Kulolo

5 cups mochiko
2-1/2 cups water
1 box brown sugar
1 can coconut milk (12-oz)
1 teaspoon baking soda

Mix ingredients together until smooth. Pour into greased 9 x 13 inch pan. Bake at 350° for 1 hour.

Jell-O Mochi

4 cups mochiko (2 10-oz pkgs)
2 pkgs Jell-O (3-oz each), any flavor desired
2 cups sugar
3 teaspoons baking powder
2 cans soda water, same flavor as Jell-O
3 eggs, beaten
1/2 cup butter, melted
katakuriko (potato starch) for sprinkling

Combine dry ingredients. Add unchilled soda water, eggs and butter. Mix well. Pour into greased 9 x 13 inch pan and bake at 350° for 1 hour. Cool and cut with a plastic knife and dust with katakuriko.

Mango with Sticky Rice

3-4 mangoes
3 cups sticky rice*
1 cup coconut milk
2-4 tablespoons sugar (to your taste)
1/4 teaspoon salt

Select mangoes firm and ripe. Chill mangoes until ready to serve. Peel and slice mangoes. Set aside. Combine rice and coconut milk and cook on medium heat for 5 minutes or until thick. Stir in sugar and salt. Reduce heat to low and simmer, covered, for 2 minutes. Serve warm with chilled mango slices.

*See "Sticky Rice" recipe on page 102.

Maui Mochi

1 pound mochiko (16-oz box)
3 cups water
1 cup White Karo (corn syrup)
1 can Koshi (12-oz can) or tsubushian (18-oz can)
katakuriko (potato starch) for dusting
red or green food color

Shape koshi or tsubushian into 1 inch balls and set aside. Refrigerate if soft.

Boil water and corn syrup. Add green or red food coloring if desired. Lower heat. Pour 1 box mochiko into syrup, stirring constantly. Mix well from bottom. Mixture will harden quickly. Mix until smooth and glossy and elastic-like texture. If it gets hard, add a little hot water.

Sprinkle katakuriko on a board and pour the cooked mochiko lengthwise. Fold over once. With a plastic knife cut 1-1/2 inch slices. Flatten slice and put tsubushian ball in the center and wrap, pinching the ends together.

Variation: Instead of Karo, substitute 1 cup sugar and 1/2 cup water.

Although it's hard work, making Maui Mochi, the end result is worth it. To make the process easier, have someone help hold the pot while stirring.

Miso Chi Chi Dango

4 cups mochiko (2 10-oz pkgs.)
3 cups sugar
1 can coconut milk (12-oz)
2 cups water
1/4 teaspoon miso
food coloring
katakuriko for dusting

Combine mochiko and sugar. Add coconut milk and water. Blend thoroughly for a smooth batter. Add 3-4 drops of food coloring and miso. Blend well. Pour into a 9 x 13 inch pan, greased or sprayed well with Pam. Cover with foil and bake at 350° for 1 hour. Cool. Cut with plastic knife and roll in katakuriko.

Mochi

yield: 8 pieces

1 cup mochiko
1 tablespoon sugar (optional)
1/4 teaspoon salt
1/2 cup water
katakuriko

Stir together mochiko, sugar and salt. Stir in water to form soft dough. Lightly knead dough on board dusted with katakuriko (about 30 seconds).

Place dough in steamer tray lined with dampened unbleached muslin or several layers of cheesecloth. Spread dough evenly over dampened cloth, about 1/2 inch thick. Steam 20 minutes. Remove steamer tray from pan. Lift out cloth with dough. Pull cloth away from dough, letting dough fall onto a flat surface dusted with katakuriko. Cool dough 1-2 minutes. While still hot, roll dough into an 8-inch long sausage-shaped roll. Cut into 8 pieces. Sprinkle with katakuriko as needed to prevent sticking. Form into balls.

Variation 1: Fill with crunchy peanut butter for peanut butter mochi.

Variation 2: For chichi dango, add 2 tablespoons melted butter and substitute 1/2 cup water with 1/2 cup milk.

Mochi Banana Bread

1 pound mochiko (16-oz box)
1 cup Bisquick®
4 teaspoons baking soda
4 teaspoons allspice or cinnamon
1 teaspoon salt
2 cups sugar

1-1/2 cups oil
3 teaspoons vanilla
5 eggs
3 cups bananas ripe & mashed
1 cup walnuts or unsalted macadamia nuts, chopped
1 cup raisins (optional)

Combine first six ingredients in large mixing bowl. Mix separately oil and vanilla and add to dry ingredients. Add eggs and mix together until batter is well blended. Stir in bananas, nuts and raisins. Pour into 4 greased loaf pans (8-1/2" x 4-1/2"). Allow batter to sit for 5 minutes before putting in oven. Bake at 350° for 1 hour or until done (when inserted knife comes out clean).

Mochi Cake

1 pound mochiko (16-oz box)
1/2 cup butter
5 eggs, beaten
1 teaspoon vanilla
3 cups milk
2-1/2 cups sugar
2 teaspoons baking powder
2 teaspoons lemon extract

Melt butter and set aside to cool. Combine mochiko, baking powder and sugar in a large mixing bowl. Combine milk, melted butter, eggs and vanilla and add to dry ingredients. Mix well until all lumps are gone and dough is smooth. Pour into buttered 9 x 13 inch pan. Bake at 350° for one hour. Cool and cut into bars.

Variation: Add 1 cup shredded or fresh frozen coconut.

Mochi Delight

1 pound mochiko (16-oz box)
2-1/4 cups sugar
1 can frozen coconut milk, thawed (12- oz)
2 cups water
food color, red or green
katakuriko or kinako for sprinkling

Combine mochiko and sugar separately. Combine coconut milk and water separately. Make a well in the dry ingredients and pour in the liquid ingredients. Mix with a wire whisk until blended. Mix in 6 drops food color of your choice. Pour into greased 9 x 13 inch pan. Cover with foil and bake at 350 degrees for 1 hour and 10 minutes. Cool for several hours or overnight. Slice into small pieces with a plastic knife and roll in katakuriko or kinako.

Mochi Dessert

2 cups mochiko (10-oz pkg)
2 cups sugar
1 tablespoon baking powder
1/4 cup butter, melted
1 can evaporated milk (12-oz)
1 can coconut milk (12-oz)
2 eggs, beaten
2 teaspoons vanilla

Combine dry ingredients. Mix well, Add remaining ingredients and blend until smooth. Pour into 9 x 13 inch pan sprayed with Pam. Bake at 350° for 45 minutes. Cool and cut into serving pieces.

Mochi Mango Nut Bread

1 pound mochiko (16-oz box)
1 cup Bisquick®
4 teaspoons baking soda
4 teaspoons allspice or cinnamon
1 teaspoon salt
1 cup granulated sugar
1 cup brown sugar

1-1/2 cups oil
3 teaspoons vanilla
1 tablespoon lemon juice
6 eggs
5 cups mangoes ripe & diced
2 cups walnuts or unsalted macadamia nuts, chopped
1 cup flaked coconut (optional)
1 cup raisins (optional)

Combine first seven ingredients in large mixing bowl. Mix separately oil, vanilla and lemon juice and add to dry ingredients. Add eggs and mix together until batter is well blended. Stir in mangoes. Add nuts, coconut and raisins. Pour into 4 greased loaf pans (8-1/2" x 4-1/2"). Allow batter to sit for 5 minutes before putting in oven. Bake at 350° for 1 hour and 15 minutes or until done (when inserted knife comes out clean).

Mochi Rice Porridge

1 pound Mochi rice
1-1/2 cups brown sugar
1 grated coconut or 1 can coconut milk (12-oz)

Wash and drain mochi rice. Cook mochi rice in rice cooker (put water just 1 inch above the rice level in the pot.) Combine brown sugar and coconut and cook until it forms into a syrup. Pour into cooked rice and stir. Mix until it forms a porridge consistency.

Mochi Rice Pudding #1

5 cups Mochi rice
1 pound dark brown sugar
3 tablespoons white sugar
1 can coconut milk (12-oz)
1 pkg shredded coconut
pinch of salt

Wash and drain mochi rice. Cook mochi rice as ordinary rice. Combine the rest of the ingredients in a large pot and bring to a boil. Add cooked rice. Stir thoroughly. Pour mochi rice mixture in a 9 x 13 inch greased pan and bake at 350° for 1 hour.

Mochi Rice Pudding #2

5 cups Mochi rice
5 cups water
1 can coconut milk (12-oz)
1 can condensed milk
brown sugar (to taste)

Wash and drain mochi rice. Cook mochi rice with 2 tablespoons coconut milk added to water. After rice is cooked, mix in desired amount of brown sugar to your taste. Spread rice in 9 x 13 buttered pan.

Topping:
Cook together coconut milk, condensed milk and 2 to 3 tablespoons brown sugar until mixture starts bubbling. Spread over mochi rice. Bake at 350° for 15 -20 minutes.

Mochi with Miso Filling

2 cups mochiko (10-oz pkg)
2/3 to 3/4 cup water
1/2 cup miso
1/2 cup sugar
ti leaf pieces (2-1/2" x 6"), oiled or sprayed with non-stick spray

Combine miso and sugar and cook over slow heat, stirring constantly until sugar is dissolved and mixture is thick. Set aside to cool.

Combine mochiko and enough water to form soft dough. Knead well. Take a piece of dough about walnut size and flatten out on palm of hand until fairly thin and oval in shape. Put a spoonful of miso filling on dough. Fold in half and pinch edges together to seal. Place on ti leaf piece and fold ti leaf over and around mochi. Steam about 20 minutes.

Mochiko Snowballs

2 cups mochiko (10-oz pkg)
2 cups flour
1-1/2 cups sugar
3 eggs
1-1/2 cups milk
1/2 teaspoon salt
4 tablespoons baking powder
oil for deep frying

Mix all ingredients together until well blended. Drop by tablespoon and fry in deep oil. Drain and sprinkle with sugar while still warm.

Nantu (Okinawan Mochi)

Step 1:
1 pound mochiko (16-oz box)
2 cups water

Mix until smooth and there are no lumps. Pour mixture in steamer lined with wet dishcloth. Steam 20-30 minutes or so until chopstick comes out clean when tested. (Mochi will look more transparent.)

Step 2:
3 cups sugar
3/4 cups water
katakuriko (potato starch) for dusting
food color, red or green

Boil sugar in water until sugar is dissolved. In a large bowl, combine the mochi and sugar mixture. Add food coloring, if desired. Mix well. Dust a 9 x 13 inch pan with katakuriko. Pour mochi into the pan. Cool. Cover with a clean dish towel and set for at least 6 hours or overnight.

Nantuyinsu (Ryukyu New Year's Pudding)

4 cups mochiko (2 10-oz pkgs)
1-1/2 cups brown sugar
1 cup miso
1 cup water
1 teaspoon black pepper
2 ti leaves
1/4 cup raw peanuts

Combine brown sugar, miso, water, mochiko and pepper in a bowl and mix thoroughly. Remove dough from bowl and knead until smooth. Divide into 3 equal parts and shape each portion into a rectangle 5 x 8 x 3/4 inch. Place each rectangle on a ti leaf. Sprinkle top with peanuts and steam for 45 minutes or until soft. Cool and cut into pieces.

Ohagi (Bota Mochi)

2 cups mochi rice
1 cup regular rice
3-1/2 cups water
1 can tsubushian (18 oz)

Rinse and soak mochi rice overnight. The next day, cook both rice together with 3-1/2 cups water. While still hot, mash rice grains partially with wooden rod or spoon dipped in water. Make rice balls about 1-1/2" diameter between palms of hands dampened with salt water. Cover rice balls with a layer of an. Makes about 24-28 balls.

Okinawa Yam Mochi

2 medium sweet potatoes
6 medium yams
2 pounds mochiko (2 16-oz boxes)
1-1/2 cups sugar
dash salt
oil for frying

Boil sweet potatoes and yams until soft and thoroughly cooked. Peel skin; mash yams and sweet potatoes together. Add mochiko gradually. Blend until texture becomes firm and manageable. Add sugar and salt; mix thoroughly. Form oblong shape (about 2-1/2" long, 1" wide and thick.) Deep fry in 375 degrees hot oil until golden brown. Drain and cool before serving.

Palitaw

2 cups mochiko (10-oz pkg.)
3/4 cup water
2-1/2 cups fresh coconut, shredded (or packaged shredded coconut)
1 tablespoon sugar
food coloring for coconut

Mix mochiko with water until a stiff dough is formed. Shape into 1-inch balls. Drop several at a time into boiling water and cook until each one floats. Remove and drain. Sprinkle with sugar and immediately coat with colored coconut.

Poi Balls

2 cups mochiko (10-oz pkg.)
2-1/2 cups sugar
1 bag poi (12-oz)
water (enough for consistency of thick pancake batter)
oil for deep frying

Combine mochiko, sugar and poi in mixing bowl. Add water gradually and blend well until mixture resembles thick pancake batter. Drop batter by teaspoonfuls in hot oil. Fry until golden brown. Drain on paper towels.

Poi Mochi

4 cups mochiko (2 10 -oz pkgs)
1-1/2 cups sugar
1 bag poi
2 cups water (more or less as necessary)
oil for deep frying

Combine mochiko, sugar and poi in mixing bowl. Add water gradually and blend well until mixture has the consistency of thick pancake batter, not watery. Drop by the teaspoon in hot oil. Fry until golden brown. Drain on paper towels.

Poi Puffs

3 cups mochiko
1 bag poi (14-oz)
1 cup water (or less)
1 cup sugar
sesame seeds
oil for deep frying

Mix the poi and water (begin with less water). Add the rest of the ingredients and mix well. Form into balls and roll in sesame seeds. Deep fry until golden brown. Drain on absorbent paper.

Pumpkin Mochi #1

yield: 4 dozen pieces

1 pound mochiko (16-oz box)
2-1/2 cups sugar
1 teaspoon baking powder
1 can pumpkin, solid pack (29-oz)
3 cups milk
1/2 cup butter, melted and cooled
5 eggs
2 teaspoons cinnamon
1 teaspoon ground ginger
1/2 teaspoon ground cloves

Combine mochiko, sugar and baking powder in large mixing bowl. In a separate bowl, beat eggs slightly. Add butter, milk, pumpkin and spices; mix well. Stir into the mochiko mixture. Mix thoroughly until smooth. Pour into greased 9 x 13 inch pan. Bake at 350° for 1 hours. Cool for several hours before cutting.

Assorted Mochi (above): Tri-Colored Mochi (Baked) page 58, Two Color Mochi page 76, Mango Mochi page 71; and Blueberry Mochi (below) page 8.

Sweet Potato Mochi, page 57.

Coconut Rice Balls (above) page 67, and Crisp Fried Shrimp (below) page 82.

Gin Doi with Char Siu Filling (above) page 30, and Iga Mochi (below) page 33.

Flavored Sticky Rice, page 106.

Fresh Strawberry Mochi, page 54.

Haum Joong (above) page 84, and Mochi Banana Bread (below) page 38.

Siu Mai with Mochi Rice, page 99.

Pumpkin Mochi #2

Dry:

1 pound + 1/4 cup mochiko (16-oz box + 1/4 cup)

2 cups sugar

2 teaspoons baking powder

1-1/2 teaspoons pumpkin-pie spice

1/2 teaspoon cinnamon

Wet:

4 eggs

1 can pumpkin, solid pack (29-oz)

1 can sweetened condensed milk (14-oz)

2 blocks butter or margarine, melted

2 teaspoons vanilla

Combine dry ingredients in large mixing bowl. In another bowl, beat eggs and add rest of wet ingredients. Combine wet and dry ingredients and mix well. Pour into greased 9 x 13 inch pan. Bake at 350° for 1 hour. Cool for 2-3 hours before cutting with a plastic knife.

Pumpkin Mochi is moist and flavorful; it's a great substitute for pumpkin pie.

Rice Cake

3 cups mochi rice
1-1/2 cups water
4 tablespoons rice wine
1-1/2 cups brown sugar

Rinse rice until water runs clear. Soak in 2 cups water for 1 hour. Drain rice and add 1-1/2 cups water and rice wine. Place mixture in electric rice cooker with 1/2 cup water in bottom of the rice cooker. (If rice cooker does not allow water in bottom, add another 1/2 cup water to rice.) When the rice cooker turns off, let rice sit, covered, for 20 minutes. Add sugar immediately and mix thoroughly. Cover rice for 5 more minutes until sugar dissolves.

Line a 8" x 8" x 1" cookie sheet with plastic wrap. Brush lightly with oil. Place rice mixture onto cookie sheet using a flat rice paddle dipped in water. Pack rice and smooth surface. Cool and cut into diamond shapes.

Sesame-Bean Paste Puffs

yield: 32 pieces

1 can koshian (12-oz)
1-1/2 pounds sweet potato or taro
2 cups mochiko (10-oz pkg)
2 tablespoons powdered sugar
3/4 cup white sesame seeds
8 cups oil for frying

Form 32 small koshian balls. Set aside. Peel sweet potato, cut into 1/3 inch slices and steam about 30 minutes until tender. Mash thoroughly. Add sugar and mochiko and mix well. Knead into a smooth dough. Roll into a long roll and cut into 32 pieces.

Roll each piece into a 2-inch flat round circle. Place 1 portion of koshian in center and gather edges of dough around filling. Pinch to seal. Roll into a cylinder shape. Dip finished puff in water and roll in sesame seeds. Heat oil for deep frying. Deep fry puffs over medium heat about 3 minutes until golden brown. Drain on paper towels.

Shiba Dango

1 pound mochiko (16-oz box)
1-1/2 cups water
1 can tsubushian (18-oz can) or koshian (12-oz can)
ti leaves, 30 cut pieces (2-1/2" x 6")

Make balls of tsubushian, the size of walnuts and set aside. Refrigerate if too soft to handle. Rub vegetable oil on ti leaf, or spray with Pam, and set aside.

Gradually add water to mochiko with chopstick. Knead dough in the bowl until bowl comes clean (wet hands if sticky). Pinch off enough dough to cover each tsubushian ball. Place mochi on ti leaf and fold leaf over and under. Can be stacked in steamer. Steam for 15 minutes

Steamed Mochi Rice with Coconut and Mango

1 pound Mochi rice
1 teaspoon vanilla
1/2 cup coconut milk, unsweetened
1 mango, ripe (diced)
1/2 teaspoon coarse ground white pepper
1/2 cup unsweetened coconut, toasted

Wash rice until water is clear. Cover rice with cold water and vanilla extract and soak overnight. Drain rice and place in steamer lined with cheesecloth. Steam on high heat for 45 minutes. (Rice should be fully cooked but not mushy.) Transfer hot rice to large bowl and add pepper, mango and coconut. Serve while hot. Top with toasted coconut, if desired.

Sticky Rice with Bananas

3 cups cooked sticky rice*
1 cup coconut milk
1/4 cup dark brown sugar
1/8 teaspoon salt
8 banana leaves, cut into 8-inch squares
3 apple bananas, cut into 1-inch strips

Combine sticky rice (* see "Sticky Rice" recipe on page 102), coconut milk, sugar and salt. Cook on medium heat until thick. Place a layer (about 3 x 3 x1/2-inch)thick of the rice mixture in the center of the banana leaf. Place a banana strip on top of the rice, then lift both ends of the banana leaf, wrapping over. Flip over so that rice goes on top of the banana in the banana leaf. Fold under the extra part of the leaf. Place in steamer and steam for 25 minutes. Serve warm or cold.

Strawberry Jell-O Mochi

4 cups mochiko (2 10-oz pkgs)
1/2 cup butter or margarine, melted
2 pkgs Strawberry Jell-O, (2 3-oz pkgs)
3 teaspoons baking soda
2 cups sugar
3 eggs, beaten
2 cans strawberry soda, room temperature
katakuriko (potato starch) for dusting
2 ti leaves, ribs removed

Mix dry ingredients first. Add eggs and butter; blend well. Add strawberry soda water last. Mix until smooth. Line 2 ti leaves on bottom of slightly greased 9 x 13 inch pan. Bake at 325° for 1 hour. Cool. Turn over on board dusted with katakuriko. Cut with plastic knife. Roll pieces in katakuriko.

(Fresh) Strawberry Mochi

1 pound mochiko (16-oz box)
3 cups water
1 cup sugar
1 can koshian
15 strawberries, whole
katakuriko (potato starch) for sprinkling

Clean strawberries, hull and pat dry. Wrap with koshian and set aside until ready to use.

Boil water and sugar. Add mochiko a little at a time and mix well. Remove from heat and place on board dusted with katakuriko and pound well. Pinch off enough dough to wrap around strawberry. Squeeze ends to seal.

Variation: Dip bottom half of strawberries in melted chocolate. Wrap mochi dough around chocolate area, allowing top of strawberry to show. Place in cupcake containers and set in muffin pan to hold its shape.

Suman

2 pounds Mochi rice

4 cups sugar

2 teaspoons vanilla

1-1/2 teaspoons salt

2 coconuts, shredded

banana leaves, cut into 8" x 10" pieces

Soak mochi rice for 3 hours. Steam in steamer lined with cheesecloth until tender. Extract milk from 2 coconuts and cook coconut milk until it becomes golden brown. Add sugar and mix well. Remove from heat and add steamed rice, mixing thoroughly. Cool. Wrap 1/2 cup mochi mixture (shaped lika a cigar) with a piece of banana leaf. Roll leaf around mochi and bend leaf at both ends to seal. Place wrapped mochi in pot. Add 1/2 cup water and bring to a boil.

Note: Clean banana leaves and place in oven, medium heat, to wilt leaves for easier wrapping.

Sweet Potato Andagi (Fried)

1 cup mochiko

1 sweet potato, peeled and boiled in little water

1/4 –1/2 cup sugar

Mash sweet potato. Add sugar and mochiko gradually and knead well. Add a little water if dough is too stiff. Spread out to rectangle of 1/2 inch thickness. Cut into wide strips of about 1-1/2 inches. Then cut strips into 1/2 inch pieces. Fry in deep oil until brown.

Sweet Potato Mochi (Baked)

yield: 24-32 pieces

1 pound mochiko (16-oz box)
1-1/2 cups brown sugar, loosely packed
1 teaspoon baking soda
1/8 teaspoon salt
1 can coconut milk (13.5-oz)
1-1/4 cups water
2 cups sweet potatoes, cooked and diced
1 tablespoon sesame seeds (optional)
katakuriko (potato starch) for sprinkling

Sift mochiko, brown sugar, baking soda and salt. Add coconut milk and water and mix well until smooth. Fold in sweet potatoes. Pour into greased 9 x 13 inch pan. Sprinkle with sesame seeds if desired. Bake for 1 hour at 350°. Cool completely before cutting. Dust with katakuriko.

Sweet Potato Mochi (Steamed)

4 cups mochiko (2 10-oz pkgs)
4 cups sweet potato, cooked and mashed
1 cup sugar (or use less)
1/2 cup water
1 can tsubushian (18-oz)
katakuriko (potato starch) for sprinkling

Mix together mochiko, sweet potato, sugar and water. Place dough into steamer lined with wet dish cloth. Steam for 15 minutes. Shape tsubushian into balls the size of walnuts and set aside. Lay the steamed mochi on cutting board sprinkled with katakuriko. Roll mochi and form a long shape. Use katakuriko as necessary. Cut pieces about 1" x 1-1/2" with plastic knife. Flatten piece of mochi and place tsubushian ball in the center. Wrap mochi around and seal. (Need to work quickly while mochi is still warm.)

Tri-Colored Mochi (Baked)

1 pound mochiko (16-oz box)
2 cups sugar
1 teaspoon baking powder
1 can coconut milk (12-oz)
2 cups water*
1 teaspoon vanilla
food color, red and green

In a large mixing bowl combine mochiko, sugar and baking powder. Blend water, coconut milk and vanilla. Add to dry ingredients gradually, mixing thoroughly with whisk or spoon.

Remove 2 cups of mixture. Add about 3 drops of green coloring. Pour into greased 9 x 13 inch pan. Cover with foil and bake 15 minutes at 350°.

Pour 2 cups white mixture over first layer. Cover with foil and bake 20 minutes.

Add red coloring to remaining mixture and pour over second layer. Cover and bake for 30 minutes. Cool uncovered, preferably overnight. Cover with clean dish cloth. Cut with plastic knife when mochi is totally cooled.

Optional: Coat mochi pieces with kinako or potato starch.

*Lessen water by 1/2 or 1/4 cup if firmer mochi is desired. If water is lessened, measure slightly less than 2 cups for each layer.

I make the Tri-Colored Mochi for Girl's Day. Very colorful. My granddaughter loves this plain without any kinako or potato starch.

Tri-Colored Mochi (Steamed)

3-3/4 cups mochiko
2-3/4 cups sugar
3 cups water
food color, red and green
katakuriko (potato starch) for sprinkling

Mix together mochiko, sugar and water. Divide batter into thirds (about 2 cups each). Add 3 drops red coloring in one third, 3 drops green in one third. Line 9 inch round pan with foil. Grease foil. Pour pink batter into pan. Cover with foil and steam for 20 minutes. Add white batter; cover and steam for 20 minutes. Add green batter; cover and steam for 40-50 minutes. Uncover and drain off water if necessary. Cool thoroughly. Cut into pieces with plastic knife and roll in katakuriko.

Tsubu An (for Mochi Filling)

yield: fills 24 mochi cakes

1 pound azuki beans
2 cups sugar
1/2 teaspoon salt

Rinse beans and soak in water overnight. Drain and place beans in pot. Add enough fresh water to cover beans. Cook until beans are soft and very tender, adding water as needed. Stir in sugar and salt. Bring to a boil, then simmer, stirring until mixture is thick and almost dry. Cool and shape into walnut-size balls.

Tsubushian Bars

6 cups mochiko
2 cups brown sugar
1 tablespoon baking soda
2 cans coconut milk (2 12-oz)
1-1/2 cups water
1 can tsubushian (18-oz)

Combine mochiko, brown sugar and baking soda. Add milk and water and mix thoroughly until batter is smooth. Mix in tsubushian.Pour into greased 9 x 13 inch pan and bake at 350° for 1 hour and 15 minutes.

Tsubushian Mochi

2 pounds mochiko (2 16-oz boxes)
1 box brown sugar
2 cans coconut milk (2 12-oz)
2 cans water (use coconut milk can)
1 can tsubushian (18-oz)
1 teaspoon baking soda

Mix all ingredients together. Pour into greased 9 x 13 inch pan. Bake at 350° for 1 hour. Cool.

White An (for Mochi Filling)

yield: fills 24 mochi cakes

1 pound lima beans
2 cups sugar
1/4 cup water (for cooking strained beans)
1/2 teaspoon salt

Prepare beans by soaking in water overnight. Next day, drain and remove outer skin. Cover beans with fresh water and boil until soft, about 30 minutes. Strain beans through wire sieve or squeeze out as much of the water as possible, using a clean cloth. Cook strained beans with sugar, 1/4 cup water and salt. Stir while cooking until mixture is almost dry. Cool and shape into walnut-size balls.

Yam-Mochiko Snowballs

4 cups mochiko (2 10-oz pkgs)
3 yams, peeled and grated (or use canned yams)
1 can coconut milk (12-oz)
2 cups sugar
6 eggs
3 tablespoons sesame seeds
oil for frying

Mix together all ingredients, except sesame seeds and oil. Form into patties and press sesame seeds into dough. Fry on both sides until golden brown.

Zenzai (Cooked Beans with Dumplings)

1 cup azuki beans
1-1/2 cups sugar
1 teaspoon salt
6-8 cups water
1 cup mochiko

Cook azuki beans with about 6-8 cups of water for about one hour. Remove from heat and cool. Drain beans and measure liquid to make 5 cups liquid. Add water if necessary. Return beans and the 5 cups liquid to stove and cook until beans are soft and tender. Add sugar and salt and bring to a boil.

Dumplings: Add enough water to mochiko to make a stiff dough. Knead dough. Pinch off small bits and roll into balls (a little larger than marbles.) Pinch each ball, making slight dents on each side. Drop one at a time into boiling bean mixture. The dumplings will rise to the top when cooked. Stir occasionally. Serve hot.

MICROWAVE *mochi*

Almond Créme Mochi

2 cups mochiko (10-oz pkg)
2-1/3 cups sugar
1 cup water
1 cup evaporated milk (12-oz)
1-1/2 teaspoons almond extract
katakuriko (potato starch) for sprinkling

Combine all ingredients, except katakuriko and mix well. Pour into 3-quart microwaveable pan, sprayed with Pam. Cover with plastic wrap and microwave on HIGH for 10-12 minutes, or until mochi has a dry surface and transparent appearance. Remove cover and use paper towel to absorb any liquid formed by steam. Cool. Turn mochi onto board dusted with katakuriko. Use a plastic knife to cut mochi. Roll pieces in katakuriko.

An Mochi

2-1/2 cups mochiko
1-1/4 cups brown sugar
1 teaspoon baking powder
1 can coconut milk (12-oz)
2 cups water
3/4 cup koshian

Mix all ingredients until smooth and well blended. Pour into large greased microwave tube pan. Microwave MEDIUM HIGH for 15 minutes. Cool.

Banana Cream Pudding Mochi

1 cup mochiko
1/2 cup sugar
2 tablespoons Instant banana cream pudding and pie filling
1 cup water
1 teaspoon vanilla
katakuriko (potato starch) for sprinkling

Combine all ingredients, except katakuriko. Mix well. Pour into microwave tube pan, greased or sprayed with vegetable spray. Cover with plastic wrap. Microwave on HIGH for 5 minutes. Rotate pan several times during cooking. Immediately remove plastic wrap and cool. Pull mochi from sides of pan and invert onto board dusted with katakuriko. Cut into 1/2 inch pieces and roll in katakuriko.

Butter Mochi Bars

1 cup mochiko
1/2 cup sugar
1/2 teaspoon baking powder
1 cup milk
2 tablespoons butter
1/4 teaspoon vanilla
kinako for sprinkling

Put butter in 8 inch square glass baking dish. Microwave for 30 seconds or until butter melts. In a mixing bowl, combine mochiko, sugar and baking powder. Add milk, vanilla and melted butter. Mix thoroughly until smooth. Pour into the glass baking dish and cook 4 minutes on HIGH. Turn the dish and microwave for 3 more minutes. Cool and cut into squares. Dust with kinako.

Chi Chi Mochi

1-1/2 cups mochiko
1/2 cup sugar
1-1/2 cups water
katakuriko (potato starch) for sprinkling

Stir ingredients together until smooth. Pour batter into buttered glass pie plate. Cook on HIGH for 9-10 minutes. Cool; cut with plastic knife. Dust with katakuriko.

Coconut Mochi

2 cups mochiko
1 can coconut milk (13.5-oz)
3/4 cup sugar
1/2 teaspoon vanilla
katakuriko (potato starch) for sprinkling

Combine mochiko, coconut milk, sugar and vanilla. Mix until smooth. Pour mixture into greased 5-cup microwave tube pan. Cover with plastic wrap. Microwave at MEDIUM HIGH for 10 minutes. Rotate pan several times during cooking. Remove from microwave and let stand a few minutes. Pull mochi from sides of pan and invert onto a board dusted with potato starch. Cool. Cut into pieces. Coat each piece with katakuriko.

Coconut Rice Balls

yield: 24 pieces

1-1/2 cups mochiko
3/4 cup boiling water
1/4 cup wheat starch
8-1/2 ounces koshian
3/4 cup coconut flakes
1 maraschino cherry, cut into small pieces for garnish
5 cups water
2-1/2 tablespoons sugar
2 tablespoons solid vegetable shortening (like Crisco)
2 tablespoons water

Step 1:

Prepare 24 koshian balls about the size of small walnuts and set aside.

Step 2:

Add 3/4 cup boiling water to the wheat starch and mix. Blend in mochiko, sugar, shortening and 2 tablespoons water. Take about 1-1/2 ounces of the dough and flatten into a pancake shape. Set aside.

Step 3:

Microwave 1 cup water in a round microwaveable container (to fit flattened dough) for 2 minutes. Place the flattened dough into the hot water and heat for another minute. Remove the dough and knead it together with the remaining dough. Divide into 24 equal portions. Wrap each portion of dough around koshian ball, seal and smooth into a ball.

Step 4:

Microwave 4 cups water for 5 minutes. Add 12 of the filled rice balls and heat 4 minutes. Remove and roll in coconut flakes. Repeat with the other 12 rice balls. Garnish each of the coconut rice balls with a tiny bit of maraschino cherry.

Easy Microwave Mochi #1

4 cups mochiko (2 10-oz pkgs)
2-1/4 cups sugar
1 can coconut milk (12-oz)
2 cups water
1 teaspoon vanilla
3-4 drops red food color

Mix all ingredients together until smooth. Grease pyrex dish; pour in batter. Place a pan of water under the pyrex dish. Cover pyrex dish with plastic wrap and microwave 20 minutes on MEDIUM HIGH. Cool before cutting.

Easy Microwave Mochi #2

2-1/2 cups mochiko
1 can coconut milk (12-oz)
1 cup brown sugar
3/4 cup water
1 teaspoon baking soda

Combine coconut milk, water and brown sugar and mix well. Stir in mochiko and baking soda and mix until smooth. Pour into buttered 8 inch baking dish. Microwave on HIGH for 15 minutes, rotating dish a quarter turn every three minutes.

Gau #1

1 pound mochiko, sifted (16-oz box)
1 pound brown brick sugar (Chinese brown sugar)
1/2 cup raw sugar (brown)
2-1/2 cups hot water
1/4 cup salad oil
2 teaspoons sesame seeds, toasted

Dissolve brick sugar and raw sugar in hot water; cool. Gradually add mochiko, stirring to make a thin batter. Stir in salad oil. Pour batter into a greased 8-cup microwave tube pan. Cover loosely with plastic wrap. Microwave at MEDIUM HIGH for 18-24 minutes. Rotate pan several times during cooking. Remove from microwave and sprinkle with sesame seeds. Let stand, uncovered for about 30 minutes. Pull gao from sides of pan and invert onto a platter.

Gau #2

1 pound mochiko (16-oz box)
1 pkg Chinese brown sugar (16-oz)
2 cups boiling water
1 can coconut milk (12-oz)
1/4 cup oil
sesame seeds

Dissolve brown sugar in boiling water. Stir in mochiko gradually. Add coconut milk and oil and beat to smooth out ingredients. Pour mixture into a 5-cup microwave tube pan sprayed with nonstick spray. Cover loosely. Microwave on HIGH for 16 minutes. Let stand 10 minutes. Sprinkle with sesame seeds.

Guava Mochi

3 cups mochiko
2 cups sugar
1-1/2 cups guava purée
1-1/2 cups water
katakuriko (potato starch) for dusting

Mix all ingredients together until smooth. Pour into greased microwave tube pan. Microwave for 14 minutes on HIGH. Cool. Slice and roll in katakuriko

Lima Bean An (for Mochi Filling)

1 pound large lima beans
2-3/4 cups sugar

Soak lima beans overnight. Remove outer skins. Add water to cover and cook until soft. Squeeze beans through clean cheesecloth. Add sugar and mix together. Microwave MEDIUM HIGH for 25 minutes. Stir every 5 minutes.

Mango Mochi

1 cup mochiko
1 pkg mango Jell-O (3-oz)
1 cup water
1 cup sugar
1 teaspoon vanilla
katakuriko (potato starch) for sprinkling

Dissolve Mango Jell-O and sugar in hot water. Add mochiko and stir thoroughly with wire whisk. Add vanilla. Pour into 9-inch microwave tube pan, greased or sprayed with non-stick spray. Cover pan with plastic wrap. Microwave 5 minutes HIGH. Remove plastic wrap immediately and cool. Turn over on board dusted with katakuriko. Cut ring in half and straighten mochi. Slice and coat pieces with katakuriko.

Microwave Mochi #1

2 cups mochiko (10-oz pkg)
2 cups water
1 cup sugar
1 teaspoon vanilla
food color, red or green
katakuriko (potato starch) or kinako for sprinkling

Combine mochiko, water, sugar, vanilla and 2-3 drops of food coloring. Mix until smooth. Pour into a greased 9-inch square microwaveable pan or greased 5-cup microwave tube pan. Cover with plastic wrap and cook on MEDIUM HIGH for 10 minutes. Uncover carefully. Cool. Loosen mochi by running plastic knife around edges of pan. Remove onto board or cookie sheet dusted with katakuriko. Cut into small pieces. Roll in katakuriko or kinako.

Microwave Mochi #2

1-1/2 cups mochiko
1-1/2 cups milk
1 cup sugar
katakuriko (potato starch) for sprinkling

Mix ingredients well and pour into square Corning Ware, lightly greased or sprayed with vegetable spray. Cover with plastic wrap. Microwave on MEDIUM for 7 minutes, then on HIGH for 3 minutes. Cool. Turn out on cutting board dusted with katakuriko. Cut into small pieces. Roll in katakuriko.

Mochi

1 cup mochiko
1/4 teaspoon salt
1 tablespoon sugar (optional)
1/2 cup water
katakuriko

Stir together mochiko, salt and sugar. Stir in water to form soft dough. Lightly knead on surface sprinkled with katakuriko (about 30 seconds). Place in greased microwave tube pan. Cover with plastic wrap and microwave on medium-high for 10 minutes. Rest 3 minutes. Turn and cook additional 2-3 minutes or until done. Cool. Turn over on flat surface sprinkled with katakuriko and cut with plastic knife into small pieces.

Mochi Cake

2 cups mochiko (10-oz pkg)
1 cup sugar
1-1/2 cups warm water
1 tablespoon oil
1/2 cup nuts, dates, prunes, etc, (chopped and mixed together)

Mix all ingredients. Pour into greased microwave tube pan. Cover with plastic wrap. Microwave on HIGH for 8 minutes. Uncover carefully and cool.

Mochi Rice with An

1-3/4 cups Mochi rice
1 cup water
1 can tsubushian (18-oz)
katakuriko (potato starch) for sprinkling

Wash mochi rice and cover with water for at least 2 hours. Form tsubushian into small balls the size of walnuts and set aside. Refrigerate if too soft.

Drain and put rice in blender with 1 cup water. Blend until mixture resembles cornmeal.

Place rice mixture into a microwaveable bowl. Cover with plastic wrap and microwave on HIGH for 5 minutes, stirring halfway through cooking time. Turn mochi onto board dusted with katakuriko. Coat dough to keep from sticking. Cut into 12 portions with plastic knife. Flatten and place tsubushian ball in center. Form buns by pulling dough up and around filling. Pinch to seal. Flatten slightly.

Okinawa Mochi

2 cups mochiko (10-oz pkg)
3/4 cup sugar
1/8 teaspoon salt
2 cups water
1 teaspoon lemon extract
food coloring, red or green
katakuriko (potato starch) for sprinkling

Combine mochiko, sugar and salt in mixing bowl. In a smaller bowl mix water, vanilla and 3-4 drops of food coloring. Add water mixture gradually to dry ingredients and mix well. Pour into greased microwave tube pan. Seal tightly with plastic wrap. Microwave on MEDIUM HIGH for 9 minutes. Carefully remove plastic wrap and place mochi on board dusted with katakuriko. Cool before cutting. Roll pieces in katakuriko.

Pink Coconut Mochi

yield: about 4 dozen pieces

4 cups mochiko (2 10-oz pkgs)
2 cups sugar
3 tablespoons butter, melted and cooled
1 can frozen coconut milk (12-oz), thawed
2 cups water
1 tablespoon vanilla
2-3 drops red food color
katakuriko (potato starch) for sprinkling

Mix together mochiko, sugar, butter, milk, water, vanilla and food color. Blend thoroughly until smooth. Pour into greased microwave tube pan. Cover with plastic wrap. Microwave on HIGH for 15 minutes. If pan does not automatically rotate, rotate the pan after 8 minutes. Remove plastic wrap immediately, being careful of steam. Cool for 10 minutes or longer, before removing mochi from pan onto board sprinkled with katakuriko. Cut into serving pieces with plastic knife. Roll in katakuriko.

Tsubushian Mochi

1-1/2 cups mochiko
1-1/2 cups water
1/2 cup sugar
1 can tsubushian (18-oz)
katakuriko (potato starch) for sprinkling

Mix mochiko, sugar and water until smooth. Pour into slightly oiled microwave tube pan. Cover with plastic wrap and microwave on HIGH for 8 minutes. Sprinkle katakuriko on cutting board (or cookie sheet or foil). Turn over mochi onto cutting board. Cut mochi with plastic knife into twelve pieces. Flatten and put tsubushian on the mochi, covering mochi completely. Make mochi when hot.

Two Color Mochi

1 pound mochiko (16-oz box)
1 can frozen coconut milk, thawed (12-oz)
2 cups sugar
1-1/4 cups water
1 teaspoon vanilla
1 teaspoon baking powder
food color
katakuriko

Mix all ingredients together until well blended. Divide mixture into 2 equal portions. Add your choice of 3-4 drops food color to one portion. Spray microwave tube pan with non-stick cooking spray. Pour one portion into pan. Cover with plastic wrap and microwave for 6-1/2 minutes. Pour on second layer, cover with plastic wrap and microwave for 6 minutes. Remove plastic wrap carefully and cool mochi. Turn over on surface sprinkled with katakuriko. Cut into small pieces with plastic knife and coat with katakuriko.

MUCH MORE *mochi*

(Entrées)

Basic White Sauce

Step 1:

2-1/2 tablespoons mochiko

1/4 cup milk

Combine mochiko and 114 cup milk to make a smooth paste. Set aside mochiko mixture.

Step 2:

4 tablespoons butter

1-1/2 cups milk

1/4 teaspoon salt

1/8 teaspoon pepper

Over low heat melt butter in 1-1/2 cup milk, salt and pepper. Stir mochiko mixture to blend again and slowly add to heating mixture. Stir until thickened.

Bread Machine Mochiko Bread

yield: 1 loaf

1 cup plus 2 tablespoons water

2 tablespoons butter, softened

2 cups bread flour

1/3 cup mochiko

3 tablespoons sugar

1 teaspoon salt

1-1/2 teaspoons powdered milk

1-1/2 teaspoons active dry yeast

Place all ingredients in pan of bread machine in the order listed. Bake according to bread machine instructions.

Boneless Stuffed Chicken Wings

2 pounds chicken wings (about 12 wings)
1/2 quantity "Flavored Sticky Rice"*

Marinade:
3 tablespoons soy sauce
1 tablespoon sugar
1 tablespoon mirin (sweetened rice wine)
1 teaspoon chopped garlic
1 teaspoon chopped fresh ginger

Basting sauce:
1 tablespoon soy sauce
1 tablespoon mirin

Debone chicken wings by removing tip and 2 bones. Rub boneless chicken wings with marinade and let stand 1 hour. Prepare 1/2 recipe of "Flavored Sticky Rice" and stuff cavity of chicken wings. Line roasting pan with foil. Place stuffed wings on foil and roast at 375° for 30 minutes. Baste with basting sauce during baking.

Note: Bake for 45 minutes if chicken is cold.

*See "Flavored Sticky Rice" recipe on page 106.

Char Siu Mochi Pudding

3 cups mochiko
1/4 cup salad oil
2 teaspoons sesame seed oil
1/4 cup cornstarch
2-1/3 cups water or chicken broth
1/2 cup char siu, coarsely minced
1/4 cup dried shrimps, washed and chopped
1 teaspoon salt
dash of white pepper
2 tablespoons green onions, cut fine
1 teaspoon sesame seeds, toasted

Put oils in large bowl. Gradually stir in mochiko, then cornstarch. Add water gradually and stir to mix thoroughly. Batter should be fairly thick and smooth. Stir-fry char siu and shrimps with salt and pepper for 1 minute. Add green onions. Add to batter and mix well.

Pour into greased 11 x 7-1/4 inch pan. Sprinkle sesame seeds over batter. Place in oven. Also place a pan of water on lower shelf. Bake at 350°. After 30 minutes, cover with foil. Bake for 30 minutes more and then turn off oven. Cook in remaining heat for 15 minutes. (Total cooking time 1-1/4 hours.) Cool.

Chicken Soup with Mochi

1 gobo (burdock)
3 shiitake mushrooms
6 cups chicken broth
1 tablespoon dashi-no-moto
1/2 pound chicken, deboned and cut into bite-size pieces
1 carrot, cut into matchstick pieces
1 teaspoon salt
1 tablespoon shoyu
Kamaboko, sliced thinly
2 green beans, parboiled and sliced diagonally
12 mochi, small (cut into pieces if large)

Scrape gobo; shave into matchstick pieces and soak in water to prevent discoloration. Rinse shiitake and soak in water to soften (save mushroom water to add to soup). Remove stems and slice shiitake thinly.

Bring chicken stock to boil. Add dashi-no-moto, chicken, gobo, shiitake and carrot. Cook until chicken is done. Season with salt and shoyu. Simmer for 10 minutes

If mochi is fresh, arrange mochi, kamaboko and beans in individual bowls. Pour in hot soup just before serving. If mochi is hard, drop into soup to soften or cook separately in hot water in small saucepan.

Crisp Fried Shrimp

Step 1:

1 pound shrimp or prawns

Remove shell but retain tail. Set aside

Step 2:

1/4 cup mochiko

2 tablespoons cornstarch

1/2 teaspoon sugar or honey

3 cloves garlic, chopped fine

1 tablespoon Chinese parsley, chopped fine

1 stalk lemon grass, chopped fine (or 1 tablespoon lemon zest)

1 teaspoon red chili peppers, seeded and chopped fine

1 teaspoon shoyu

1 teaspoon fish sauce or 1/2 teaspoon salt

1 egg

1/4 teaspoon black pepper

1/4 cup cold water

Combine all ingredients, except cold water,and blend well. Stir in cold water and mix well.

Step 3:

Preheat enough oil for deep-frying on medium heat. Coat shrimp with mochiko mixture. Deep fry until golden brown. Drain on paper towels.

Crispy Fried Chicken

2 pounds chicken drummettes
3 tablespoons mochiko
2 teaspoons brown sugar
2-4 tablespoons fish sauce (or 2 teaspoons salt)
3 stalks lemon grass, chopped fine (or 3 tablespoons lemon zest)
5 cloves garlic, chopped fine
2 tablespoons oil
1/2 teaspoon black pepper
3 tablespoons chopped Chinese parsley,

Combine all ingredients, except chicken. Mix well and marinate chicken in refrigerator overnight. Heat enough oil for deep frying on medium heat until oil is hot. Fry chicken until cooked, about 15 minutes. Remove and drain on paper towels. Let cool before serving.

Note: One tablespoon of lemon zest (grated lemon peel) has the same flavor intensity of 1 tablespoon chopped fresh lemon grass.

Haum Joong

1-1/2 pounds belly pork

Slice belly portk into 30 pieces (2-1/2" x 3"). Combine 1-1/4 teaspoons salt and 1/4 teaspoon five spice and rub gently into pork. Cover and put in refrigerator for 2-3 days.

3 pound mochi rice

Wash and drain mochi rice well through a colander. Mix 2-1/2 quarts water and 2-3/4 tablespoons Hawaiian salt. Add drained rice and stir well. Add enough water to cover rice and let stand for 10 hours. When done, drain.

20 salted duck eggs

Use only yolks of salted duck eggs. Cut into halves.

20 ti leaves

Cut off both ends of ti leaf allowing 12" in length. Wash clean. To soften leaves, place in pot, add water to cover and simmer for 30 minutes. When done, drain and soak in cold tap water, changing water until water is clear and odor is gone (about 8 hours). Drain. Rub oil on top of leaves.

Wrapping:

Place 2 leaves, with oil side up, alternating stem end and tip end. Overlap leaves 3" deep. Put 1/2 cup prepared rice in the center; then line 4 halves of yolks evenly on top. Place 3 pieces of seasoned pork on yolks. Add another 1/2 cup rice over. Fold the side of the top leaf over the rice first, then the side of the bottom leaf over it. Fold over both ends (stem and tip ends). Tie crisscross with cotton string.

continued on next page...

continued from previous page

Boiling Wrapped Rice:

Place wrapped rice in a large pot; add 3 tablespoon Hawaiian salt. Pour boiling water over to cover, 2-3 inches above rice. Bring water to boil. Cover and cook for about 6 hours. Water should always be at a low boil. Add boiling water every 2 hours to cover rice. When done, take out and drain. Cool before slicing.

Ip Jai (Steamed Mochi Dumplings)

Filling:

1/3 cup roasted peanuts, chopped
2/3 cup shredded coconut (unsweetened)
1-1/2 teaspoons sesame seeds, toasted
4 teaspoons sugar

Wrapper:

2 cups mochiko (10-oz pkg.)
3/4 to 1 cup water
5 ti leaves cut into 3 x 4 inch pieces and oiled with salad oil
cotton twine to wrap the dough in the leaves (optional)

Combine filling ingredients and set aside.

Mix mochiko and water to make a crumbly dough. Divide dough into 12 parts. Press each part into a circle, about 3 inches in diameter. Place 1 tablespoon filling in center of each circle of dough and pinch edges of dough together to seal and form a ball. Wrap each ball in a piece of oiled leaf. Place in an oiled steamer and steam for 20 minutes.

Mochi Balls in Soup

Step 1:

1-1/2 cups mochiko

1/2 cup cooked ham, finely minced

1-1/2 teaspoons salt

pepper to taste

2/3 cup chicken broth

Combine mochiko, ham and salt and mix together. Add broth gradually to make dough. Pinch dough to form 1/2 inch mochi balls.

Step 2:

2 cups ground pork

1 tablespoon Chung choi, minced

1/4 cup water chestnuts, chopped

1 tablespoon cornstarch

1 teaspoon shoyu

1 tablespoon oil

salt and pepper to taste

Combine all ingredients. Mix well. Form into 1/2 inch pork balls.

Step 3:

2 tablespoons oil

1/2 cup dried shrimps, washed and soaked for 1/2 hour

dash of salt to taste

2 quarts hot water

4 cubes chicken bouillon

1-1/2 cups turnip, cut julienne

green onions, chopped fine

Chinese parsley, chopped fine

Heat oil in large saucepan. Add salt and shrimps. Stir-fry 10 seconds. Add hot water. Add bouillon. Boil to dissolve cubes. Add pork balls to

continued on next page...

continued from previous page

soup and cook for 5 minutes. Add turnip strips and cook until tender. Add mochi balls and cook for 3-4 minutes until balls float to the top. Season soup to taste. Serve with cut green onions and Chinese parsley.

Variation: Use other vegetables (Chinese cabbage, Chinese squash, or mustard cabbage.)

Mochi Duck

Step 1:

4 pounds duck

4 tablespoons shoyu

2 tablespoons sherry

1 tablespoon honey

2 teaspoons salt

1/2 cup green onions, chopped fine

4 slices ginger, minced

Have butcher debone duck with shape and skin intact. Combine rest of the ingredients and marinate duck for 1 hour. Drain duck, reserving sauce, and pat dry with paper towels. Hang in a cool airy place for 2 hours or use an electric fan. Place dripping pan under duck.

Step 2:

1-1/2 cups Mochi rice

Wash rice and drain. Soak in water for 1 hour and drain. Cook in rice cooker with 1-1/2 cups water

Step 3:

2 tablespoons oil

1/4 cup baby dried shrimps, soaked

1/2 cup smoked ham, diced

1/2 cup lup chong, cooked and diced

1/4 cup green onions, chopped fine

1/4 cup Chinese parsley, chopped fine

Heat oil in frying pan. Stir-fry shrimps first, then add rest of ingredients. Add reserved sauce and let sizzle. Add cooked mochi rice and mix well.

continued on next page...

continued from previous page

Step 4:

Stuff duck. Sew up the tail opening and secure. Heat 3 cups oil until very hot. Deep fry duck until golden brown. Remove duck and drain. Cool duck slightly.

Reheat oil until very hot. Deep fry for 1 minute to keep skin crispy.

Mochi Rice Pilaf

3 cups uncooked mochi rice

4 links lup chong

1 can chicken broth (13-oz) plus water to make 3 cups liquid

1 teaspoon salt

Rinse rice and drain. Steam lup chong for 20 minutes. Drain off oil and cut into half-inch chunks.

In rice cooker put alternate layers of rice and lap chong (3 or 4 layers). Add salt to chicken broth and water liquid and pour into cooker. Cook until tender.*

Variation: Use shiitake mushrooms, dried shrimps, ham, etc.

* If rice is not quite done when cooker goes off, scoop rice into a regular pot and cook on stove over low heat.

The Mochi Rice Pilaf recipe is an easy way to cook mochi rice to taste like joong (Chinese tamale).

Mochi Rice Stuffing

2-1/2 cups mochi rice
2-1/2 cups water
6 shiitake mushrooms, soaked
3 slices bacon, chopped
1 cup round onion, chopped
1/2 cup green onions, chopped
1/2 pound lup chong, diced
1 cup water chestnuts, chopped
2 tablespoons Chinese parsley, chopped
2 teaspoons shoyu
1-1/2 teaspoons salt
1/2 teaspoon sugar
dash of pepper

Rinse mochi rice; drain. Place rice in rice cooker and add 2-1/2 cups water. Soak for 1 hour; then cook rice until tender. Remove stems from mushrooms, chop caps.

In large saucepan fry bacon until crisp; stir in onions, green onions and mushrooms. Cook until onions are clear. Add remaining ingredients and cooked rice and mix gently together.

Mochiko Chicken

2 pounds chicken thighs, deboned
4 tablespoons mochiko
4 tablespoons cornstarch
4 tablespoons sugar
5 tablespoons shoyu
2 cloves garlic, minced
1/2 teaspoon salt
2 eggs, beaten
1/4 cup green onions, chopped
1/2 teaspoon ginger, grated

Mix everything except chicken. Add chicken and marinate for 5 hours or overnight in refrigerator. Fry in 1-inch hot oil until golden brown on both sides. Serve hot or cold. When cold, may be cut into slices (similar to chicken katsu).

Oyster Chicken

1/3 cup mochiko
1 tablespoon flour
1/3 cup cornstarch
1/3 cup sugar
1/3 cup shoyu
1 egg
1 tablespoon oyster sauce
1 tablespoon sesame seeds
green onions, chopped fine
5 pounds chicken
oil for frying

Debone chicken. Combine all ingredients and marinate chicken overnight in refrigerator. Place oil in frying pan and fry chicken.

Ozoni

Step 1:

8 cups water

1/4 cup dried shrimps

4 shiitake mushrooms

1 dashi konbu, 6-inch strip

4 tablespoons shoyu

2 teaspoons salt

Soak mushrooms until softened. Remove stems and slice thinly. Set aside. Into a large pot, measure shiitake water and add enough water to make 8 cups. Add shrimps and konbu and bring to a boil. Reduce heat and simmer for 30-40 minutes. Strain out shrimps and konbu. To strained soup, add sliced shiitake, shoyu and salt and bring soup to a boil.

Step 2:

1 bunch Mizuna

8 pieces mochi

Kamaboko, cut into thin slices

Parboil mizuna; drain well and squeeze out water. Cut mizuna into 2-inch lengths. Set aside. Place fresh mochi, mizuna and kamaboko into individual bowls and pour hot soup over. Serve immediately.

If mochi has hardened, cook mochi pieces in hot water to desired softness.

Rice Cooker Osekihan

yield: 6-8 servings

2 cups mochi rice
1/3 cup azuki beans
black sesame seeds for sprinkling
salt for sprinkling

Step 1:

Rinse azuki beans. Soak in 3 cups water overnight. Next day, cook for about 10-20 minutes until beans are just tender. Do not overcook. Remove from heat and set aside to cool.

Step 2:

Rinse mochi rice until water runs clear. Soak rice in water about 1 hour. Drain; set aside in strainer. Strain azuki beans and save azuki water in a bowl.

Step 3:

Place drained mochi rice in rice cooker. Add azuki beans and level with hand. Add enough azuki water to just cover the azuki beans. Turn rice cooker on. After the cooker has turned off, let rice sit with cover on for 15 minutes. Carefully mix rice with the beans. Serve rice sprinkled with salt and sesame seeds.

Rice Covered Balls

Step 1:

1 cup mochi rice, soaked in water for 1 hour and drained.

Step 2:

1 pound ground pork
1 link lup chong, minced
1/4 cup bamboo shoots, chopped
2 shiitake mushrooms, soaked and chopped
1 tablespoon rice wine
1 tablespoon shoyu
1 teaspoon salt
2 tablespoons cornstarch
1 tablespoon sesame oil
5 water chestnuts, cut into quarters

Combine all ingredients, except for water chestnuts. Shape ground pork mixture into 1-1/2" ball, placing a piece of water chestnut in the center. Roll each meat ball in drained sweet rice. Place in steamer and steam for 25 minutes.

Rice Wrapped in Lotus Leaf

Step 1:

2 cups mochi rice, uncooked

Prepare rice so that rice is hot and ready for "Step 3." Wash rice and drain. Soak in water (covering rice completely) for 2 hours and drain. Place rice on damp cheesecloth in steamer, spreading rice evenly with a hole in center of rice for steam. Cover and steam for 40 minutes. (Makes 4 cups cooked rice.)

continued on next page...

continued from previous page

Step 2:

6 lotus leaves

1/2 pound boneless chicken, diced in cubes

Marinade for Chicken:

1/2 teaspoon ginger, grated

2 teaspoons shoyu

1/2 teaspoon sugar

1 tablespoon cornstarch

2 teaspoons sesame seed oil

Soak lotus leaves in hot water and rinse thoroughly. Pat dry. Marinade chicken and set aside.

Step 3:

1 tablespoon oil

2 links lup chong, diced

1 cup barbecued pork, diced (char siu)

1 shiitake mushroom, soaked and diced

2 tablespoons shoyu

3 tablespoons oyster sauce

2 hard boiled eggs, quartered

1/2 cup Chinese parsley

Heat pan, add oil and stir fry chicken. Add pork, sausage, mushrooms, shoyu and oyster sauce. Turn off heat and mix in hot, cooked rice. Divide rice into 6 portions. Place 1/2 of the portion of rice onto lotus leaf. Put 1 piece of egg in the center and cover with parsley. Cover with remaining portion of rice. Bring sides of leaf up and around to cover rice. Roll to enclose contents. Place wrapped rice in steamer and steam for 20 minutes.

Salty Rice Ball Soup

Step 1:

1/3 pound chopped pork

1/2 teaspoon salt

1/4 teaspoon black pepper

1 tablespoon sautéed shallots, minced

1/4 teaspoon sesame oil

1 teaspoon cornstarch

Mix chopped pork with the rest of the ingredients until thoroughly combined. Separate into 24 portions. Set aside.

Step 2:

2 cups mochiko

1/2 cup boiling water

1/2 cup cold water

Mix ingredients and knead into a smooth dough. Roll into a long roll and cut into 24 pieces. Form each piece into a ball and flatten into a 3-inch circle. Place 1 portion of filling (from step 1) in center of circle and gather edges of circle around filling. Pinch to seal and roll into balls.

Step 3:

6 pieces green onions (1-inch each)

4 tablespoons oil

9 cups water

2-1/2 cups salt

1/4 teaspoon sesame oil

1/4 teaspoon black pepper

1/2 teaspoon spinach or watercress, cut into 1-inch sections

Heat pan and add oil. Stir-fry onion sections and add all ingredients, except spinach. Heat liquid until boiling and add rice balls. Bring to boil and cook 5 minutes over medium heat. When balls float to surface, add spinach and let boil again. Serve in bowls.

Salty Rice Dumplings

Filling 1:

2 tablespoons small dried shrimps, rinse and chop coarsely, add 1/2 teaspoon water and soak 1/2 hour

1/3 ball chung choi, rinse, chop fine

3 shiitake mushrooms, soak until soft. Remove stems, squeeze, chop coarsely

2 water chestnuts, chop coarsely

3/4 teaspoon sugar

1-1/4 teaspoons oyster sauce

2 tablespoons chicken broth

2 tablespoons green onions, slice fine

1 tablespoon chinese parsley, chopped fine

Filling 2:

3 tablespoons smoked ham, chopped coarsely

1/3 cup roast pork, chop coarsely

2 tablespoons peanut oil

salt to taste

Heat pan, add oil; bring to high heat, then remove pan to cool slightly. Return pan to low heat and stir-fry ham and roast pork for 30 seconds. Add filling #1, stir well, cover and simmer for 2 minutes. Cool.

Preparing Dumplings:

1/2 pound mochiko

1/3 teaspoon salt

10-1/2 tablespoons water

Mix mochiko and salt. Moisten mochiko mixture with water and stir with a spoon to form dough. Knead until smooth. Roll dough into 1-1/4" diameter. Cut into 16 pieces. Shape into balls. Press thumb in center to make a cavity. Then press onto cups until dough is 1/8" thick. Fill with 2 teaspoons of filling. Press filling firmly. Pinch ends to seal.

continued on next page...

continued from previous page

Boiling Dumplings:

7-1/2 cups water

1/2 teaspoon salt

In large pot, add water and salt; stir. Boil. Put dumplings in and bring to a boil again; then lower heat to low. Cook until dumplings float to top. Stir dumplings around gently to cook evenly. Scoop out when done, and drain.

Note: Place any remaining filling on a plate, spreading it evenly. Serve dumplings on this prepared plate, or sprinkle filling over dumplings.

Sekihan

yield: 6-8 servings

2 cups Mochi rice

1/2 cup regular rice

1/2 cup Azuki beans

2-1/2 cups water (including azuki water)

red food coloring

salt to taste

sesame seeds for sprinkling over rice

Rinse azuki beans. Add enough water to cover and soak for 2 hours. Cook at medium heat for about 40 minutes. Remove pot from heat and let stand for about 30 minutes. Drain and keep stock. Add stock to water to make 2-1/2 cups liquid. Try to keep beans from breaking.

Rinse rice. Add 2-1/2 cups liquid, 2 drops red food color, and azuki beans. Mix well. Let stand 30 minutes. Cook in automatic rice cooker. During cooking, the beans will float to the surface. When ready to serve, carefully stir to mix the beans with the rice. Serve into rice bowls and sprinkle with salt and black sesame seeds.

Siu Mai with Mochi Rice

Step1:

1-1/2 cups Mochi rice

Rinse rice until water runs clear; drain. Soak rice covered with water for 1 hour; drain. Place rice and 1-3/4 cup water in small pot and boil 3 minutes over high heat. Turn heat to low and cook 7 minutes. When done, remove rice into container and toss rice lightly.

Step 2:

2 tablespoons oil
1 cup cooked pork loin, diced (or char siu)
1/4 cup shiitake mushrooms, soaked and diced
1/4 cup dried shrimp, diced
1/2 tablespoon rice wine
2 tablespoons shoyu
1/2 teaspoon salt
1 teaspoon sugar
1/4 teaspoon black pepper

Heat pan; add oil. Stir-fry diced pork, mushrooms and shrimp. Add the rest of the ingredients and cooked mochi rice and mix together.

Step 3:

36 won ton skins
2 tablespoons green oinions, chopped
2 tablespoons chopped egg sheet*

Trim won ton skins to circles. Place a portion of the rice mixture in the middle of each won ton circle. Gather edges up to form a cup-shape. Keep top open. Squeeze slightly in the middle of the cup-shape to form a "waist." Smooth top with the underside of a spoon and sprinkle green onions and chopped egg sheet on top. Place siu mai in steamer and steam 3 minutes over high heat.

continued on next page...

continue from previous page

* To prepare egg sheet, beat 3 eggs and fry in oiled pan. Tilt pan to distribute egg evenly. Cook over low heat until firm. Flip over egg sheet and cook briefly. Remove, cool and chop thinly.

Steamed Mochi Rice with Pork Filling

Step 1: Rice Mixture

3 cups Mochi rice, uncooked
1 cup regular rice, uncooked
1 cup water
2 cans chicken broth
1 cube chicken bouillon
1 tablespoon dried chives

Rinse rice; drain. Soak for 1 hour; drain. Measure chicken broth and water to make 4-1/2 cups liquid. Combine liquid, rice, bouillon and chives and cook in rice cooker.

Step 2: Pork Filling

1/2 cup cooked ham, diced
1 cup cooked larp chong, diced
1/2 cup char siu, diced
1/2 cup shiitake mushrooms
1/2 cup green onions, chopped fine

Soak shiitake mushrooms in water until soft. Discard stems. Slice very thin and boil in water for 10 minutes. Drain and squeeze excess water.

Step 3:

Combine pork filling with cooked rice and mix well.

Steamed Vegetable Dumplings

Step 1:

3-1/2 pounds turnip

1 teaspoon salt

1/3 pound bacon, chopped

2 stalks green onions, chopped

1/4 cup dried shrimp, chopped

4 tablespoon oil

salt to taste

dash of pepper

Peel turnip and grate fine. Add salt and soak 15 minutes; drain. Heat pan and oil. Stir-fry bacon over high heat. Add green onions and shrimp. Continue to stir-fry. Add turnip, salt and pepper and stir-fry to mix together. Remove; cool. Separate into 20 portions.

Step 2:

3 cups mochiko

1/2 cup flour

2/3 cup boiling water

1/3 cup cold water

1 tablespoon solid vegetable shortening (like Crisco)

Sift mochiko and flour. Add boiling water; mix well. Add cold water; mix well. Add vegetable shortening; knead to a smooth dough and cut into 20 pieces.

Step 3:

20 pieces lettuce or cabbage leaves cut into round circles

Flatten dough pieces into circles. (Add a little oil if sticky.) Place turnip filling in middle and fold over and seal. Place each finished dumpling on a lettuce leaf and steam for 10 minutes over high heat.

Sticky Rice (Steamed Mochi Rice)

yield: about 2 cups cooked rice

1 cup mochi rice, uncooked

Rinse rice; drain. Repeat until water runs clear. Soak overnight covered completely with water. Drain. Spread rice evenly in a steamer lined with damp cheesecloth. Steam 40-45 minutes over boiling water until tender and translucent. Remove from heat and toss lightly. Serve hot.

Stir-Fried Mochi Rice

yield: serves 4-5 as a main course

1 pound mochi rice
1 ounce dried shrimps, rinsed
10 shiitake mushrooms
1 lup chong, diced
1 Chinese duck liver sausage, diced
2 tablespoons peanut oil
4 stalks green onions, cut fine, divided
6 ounces roast pork, diced
1 tablespoon thick soy sauce
1 teaspoon salt
Chinese parsley, chopped

Step 1:

Rinse mochi rice; drain. Soak in water for 6 hours or overnight. Drain just before use. Soak shrimps in boiling water (just enough water to cover) for 20 minutes. Drain, saving the liquid. Soak shiitake in 1/2 pint water until soft. Drain, saving the soaking liquid. Squeeze out excess water and dice mushrooms.

Step 2:

Heat a wok over high heat until smoking. Add oil and swirl around. Add sausages and shrimp; turn and toss for 1 minute. Add mushrooms, continue to stir-fry. Add rice, turning and tossing rice. Sprinkle on 2-3 ounces of shrimp/mushroom water; cover. Continue to cook over medium to low heat for 2 minutes. Sprinkle liquid again, fold and turn the rice 5 or 6 times; then cover some more. Repeat this procedure 4 more times using ordinary water when the shrimp/mushroom water is used up.

Add salt, 1/2 of the chopped green onions and roast pork. Flip and turn to mix. Repeat the sprinkling of water and simmering another 3 or 4 times, each time for about 4 or 5 minutes. Continue to simmer until rice is cooked. Add water as necessary. Remove from heat and fold in remaining green onions, Chinese parsley and soy sauce. Serve hot.

Tasty Chicken Thighs

4 pounds chicken thighs or wings
4 tablespoons mochiko
4 tablespoons cornstarch
2 tablespoons flour
4 tablespoons sugar
1-3/4 teaspoons salt
5 tablespoons shoyu
1 teaspoon oyster sauce
2 eggs
2 stalks green onions, chopped
1 tablespoon sesame seeds

Mix all ingredients except the chicken. Pour over chicken and marinate for two hours. Fry slowly in oil.

Three Topping Rice

yield: 4-6 servings

Step 1: Rice

2-1/2 cups rice
1/2 cup mochi rice
3 cups water
2 tablespoons sake (Japanese rice wine)
1 teaspoon salt
2-3 drops red food color

Rinse rice and mochi rice until water runs clear; drain. Mix in rest of ingredients and cook in rice cooker.

continued on next page...

continued from previous page

Step 2: Green Topping

1 box frozen peas (10-oz)

1 cup water

1/2 teaspoon salt

1 teaspoon sugar

Bring water to boil. Add peas; cook 2 minutes and drain. Stir in sugar and salt. Cook on low heat until liquid is absorbed. Set aside.

Step 3: Pink Topping

1 can small shrimps (7 to 8 oz can), drained

2 tablespoons sugar

2-3 drops red food color

Mince shrimps as finely as possible. Place in saucepan with sugar and red food color and cook over low heat, stirring constantly until flaky. Set aside.

Step 4: Yellow Topping

5 eggs

1/2 teaspoon salt

3 tablespoons sake (Japanese rice wine)

1 teaspoon sugar

oil for frying

Break eggs into a bowl. Mix well with seasonings. Heat oil in saucepan and cook eggs on medium heat, stirring constantly until dry.

Step 5:

Nori (seaweed sheets), toasted, crushed

Red pickled ginger, slivered

Fill individual bowls 3/4 full with rice. Cover rice with peas, shrimps and eggs in three sections. Garnish with nori and pickled giner.

Flavored Sticky Rice

Step 1:

1/2 cup shiitake mushrooms, soaked and diced

1 link larp chong, diced

1 cup char siu

1 tablespoon oil

Heat wok (or frying pan). Add oil and heat until hot; stir-fry on medium heat, mushrooms, larp chong and pork.

Step 2:

2 tablespoons shoyu

1 tablespoon oyster sauce

1 tablespoon rice wine

1 tablespoon sesame oil

1/2 teaspoon sugar

1/8 teaspoon white pepper

2 cups steamed mochi rice*

Add all ingredients, except mochi rice and fry together. Stir in rice combining everything thoroughly. Place in individual bowls suitable for steaming and steam for 15 minutes.

Note: Can be made ahead and steamed just before serving. Also a delicious stuffing for chicken.

* See "Sticky Rice" recipe on page 102

Vegetable Mixed Rice

yield: 6-8 servings

4 cups mochi rice

1 package (6 to8 oz) sansai mix (mountain vegetables) rinsed and drained

4 shiitake mushrooms, soaked and slivered

6 kikurage (cloud ear fungus), soaked and chopped

1 konnyaku, cut into small irregular pieces with spoon

1/2 cup gobo, cleaned and slivered (soak in water to prevent discoloration)

1 aburage, cut into small pieces

Stock:

2-1/2 cups water

2 tablespoons bonito stock base

2 tablespoons soy sauce

2 tablespoons mirin (sweetened rice wine)

1 teaspoon salt

Rinse mochi rice until water runs clear; drain. Soak mochi rice in stock for 5 hours or more. Drain rice and save stock for sprinkling over rice while steaming. Mix rice with rest of ingredients and place in steamer lined with cheesecloth. Steam rice mixture for 40 minutes, sprinkling stock over rice, once or twice.

GLOSSARY

Aburage	Deepfried bean curd
An	Paste made from beans, used to fill confections
Azuki	Small red beans
Cascaron	Fried mochi-coconut balls
Char siu	Roasted sweet red pork
Chi chi	Milk
Chung choi	Salted turnip or radish
Daikon	White radish or turnip
Dashi	Soup stock
Dashi Konbu	Dried seaweed (kelp) used for soup stock
Dashi-no-moto	Soup stock base (powder)
Dango	Dumpling
Gobo	Burdock root
Goma	Sesame seed
Haupia	Coconut cornstarch pudding
Hokkigai	Clam
Hung jo	Chinese dried red date
Joong	Chinese tamale
Kamaboko	Steamed fish cake
Karabasa	Pumpkin
Katakuriko or Katakuri	Potato starch
Kinako	Ground roasted soybean flour
Konbu	Dried kelp, seaweed
Koshian	Smooth bean paste

Larp chong or Lup chong	Chinese sausage
Lilikoi	Passion fruit
Miso	Paste of fermented rice and soybeans
Mochi	Glutinous rice or sweet rice flour
Mochiko	Glutinous rice flour
Nantu	Steamed Okinawan mochi
Poi	Steamed and mashed taro
Sekihan	Mochi rice with red bean
Shiitake	Black mushrooms, usually available dried
Shoyu	Seasoning sauce made from soy beans, soy sauce
Ti	Cordyline termenalis. Large oblong leaves used in wrapping food for cooking
Tsubushian	Coarsely ground red bean paste
Yomogi	Mugwort, dark green leaves used to color and flavor mochi or used as a herb
Konnyaku	yam cake
Kikurage	cloud ear fungus
Mirin	sweet rice wine
sake	Japanese rice wine

Index